HOW TO DRAW WITH PASTELS

Macdonald

CONTENTS

HOW TO USE THIS BOOK

Here are step-by-step demonstrations of a range of subjects designed to illustrate some ways of using pastel. To get the most out of these exercises, study each one first and then either re-paint or re-draw it yourself, or apply the techniques to a subject or scene of your own choice.

Copying — Don't be concerned about copying the exercises — many famous artists have borrowed ideas and painting techniques and have used them to develop their own individual style. Copying the exercises will make learning the techniques easier as you won't have to worry about finding a subject, composition or design.

Stay loose — Attack each painting or drawing vigorously and don't worry about making mistakes — the more you practise and experiment, the sooner you will see a dramatic improvement in your painting.

Experiment — Attack the subject boldly — taking risks with lines, colour, shapes and values will prevent your work looking tight and overworked. Apply colour freely and don't hold the stick too tightly or your work will look tentative. Start loosely, saving the detailed work for the finishing touches.

Keep it simple — Select simple subjects and compositions to start with. Restrict the number of colours you use and avoid overworking them. If you follow these simple rules you will soon produce surprisingly good paintings and then you can really start to experiment with more ambitious compositions and colour schemes and develop your own unique painting style.

Happy painting!

A MACDONALD BOOK

First published in Great Britain in 1986
by Macdonald & Co (Publishers) Ltd
London & Sydney

A member of BPCC plc

How to draw with pastels
The Macdonald Academy of Art
1. Pastel drawing — Technique
I. Series
741.2'35 NC880

ISBN 0 356 12350 2

This book was designed and produced by
Quintet Publishing Limited
6 Blundell Street, London N7

Typeset in Great Britain by
Facsimile Graphics Limited, Essex
Colour origination in Hong Kong by
Hong Kong Graphic Arts Limited, Hong Kong
Printed in Hong Kong by Leefung-Asco
Printers Limited

Macdonald & Co (Publishers) Ltd
Greater London House
Hampstead Road
London NW1 7QX

MATERIALS

Pastels are powdered pigments mixed with just enough gum or resin to bind them together. The word pastel is derived from the resulting 'paste', which is moulded into the familiar pastel sticks. The charm and freshness of pastels, their purity of colour and their immediate response when applied to paper are part of the nature of the medium and distinguish it from oil painting. Pastels can be purchased in three qualities, soft, medium and hard. Soft pastels offer the most brilliant range of colours.

Unlike watercolour and oils, pastels cannot be mixed on the palette to form other colours and tones. These have to be manufactured separately, and, in all, some 600 tints are on the market. Some manufacturers supply pastels in pencil form. Selecting a suitable range is very much a matter of individual taste. A basic selection might consist of about 48 colours, while a small range of about twelve colour sticks would be suitable for outdoor sketching. Begin with a boxed set and expand the selection as needed.

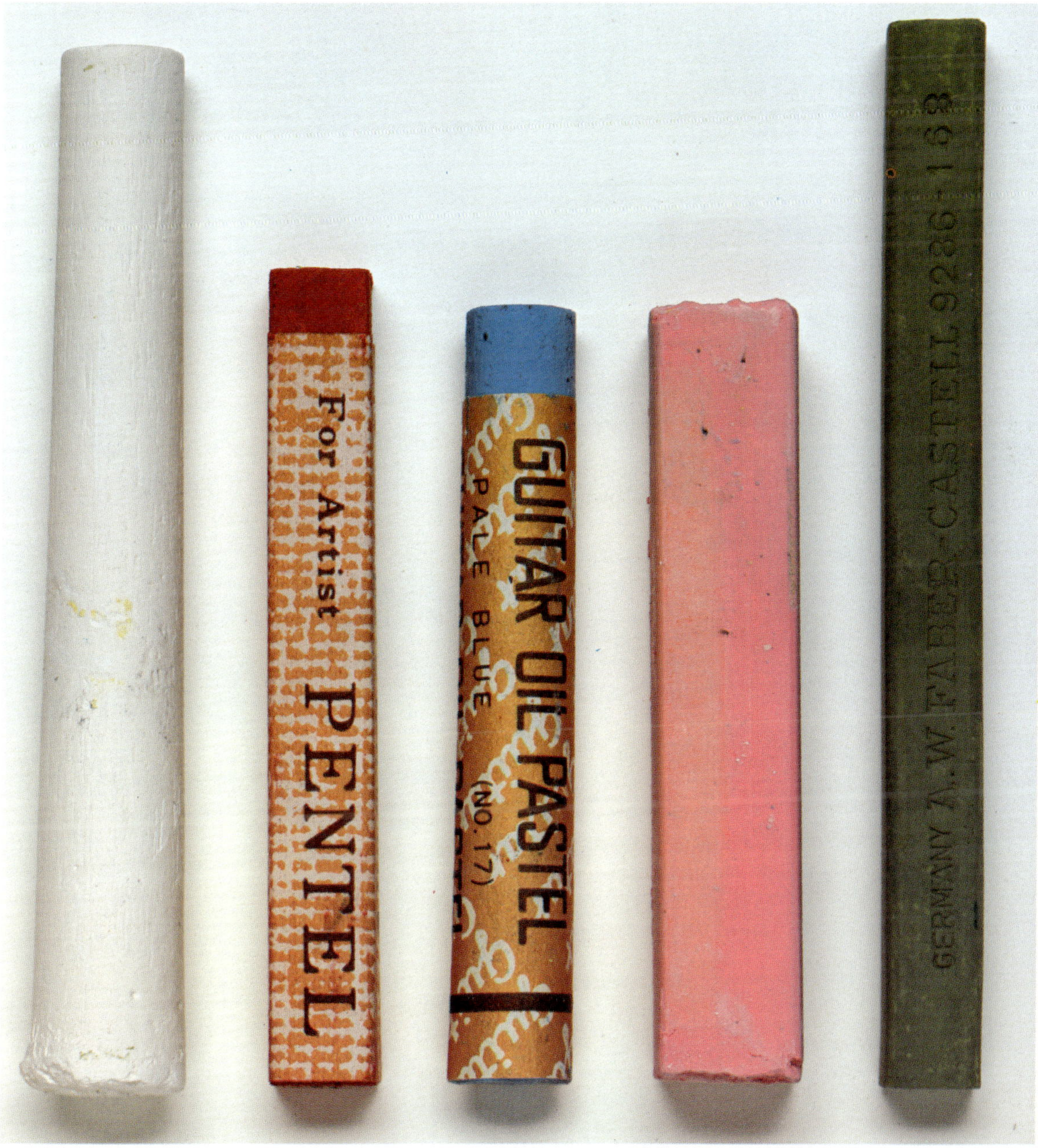

TECHNIQUES

Before beginning a picture, lay out your pastels on a piece of soft cloth or corrugated cardboard, arranging them carefully according to colour and tone. In this way you will avoid having to break off in the middle of the work to search for the right colour pastel.

Begin by practising various strokes, colours and effects on paper similar to that to be used for the picture itself. You will find that the pastel stick can be manipulated to produce thick and thin lines and textures. For instance, the sharp edge of a broken pastel, drawn lightly across the paper, will produce a fine line; by laying the end of the pastel flat on the paper a flat even area of colour can be laid down. Heavy pressure forces a lot of pastel into the grain of the paper, light pressure reveals more paper through the colour. Pastel laid on flock paper gives a velvety patch of colour, on fine canvas it produces a fairly flat colour. On glass paper and ingres paper much of the texture shows through the pastel.

Delicate contrasts can be achieved by covering a torchon or stiff brush with powdered pastel and applying it lightly across the picture. Fine hatching, cross-hatching or alternatively strokes of different colours and tones produce effective shading.

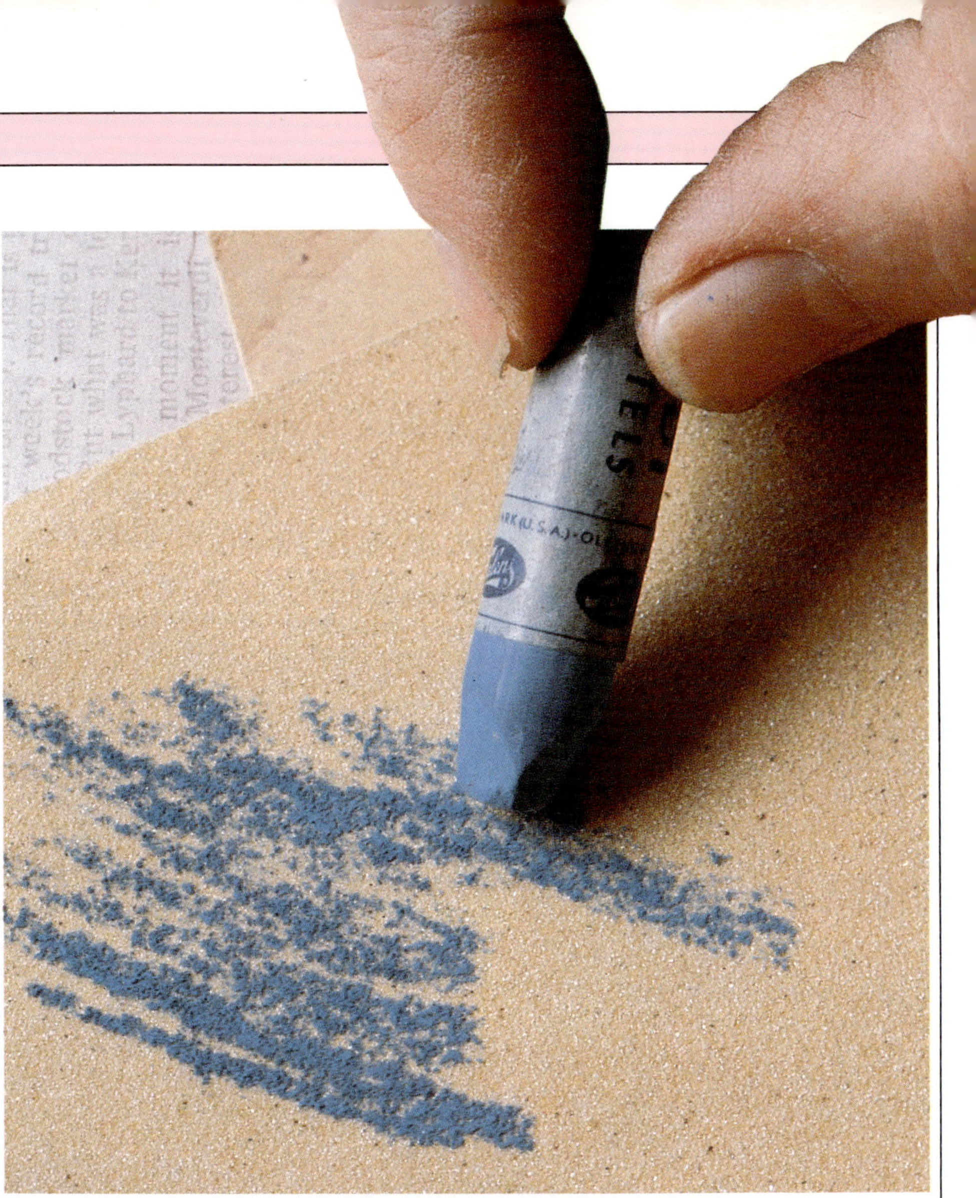

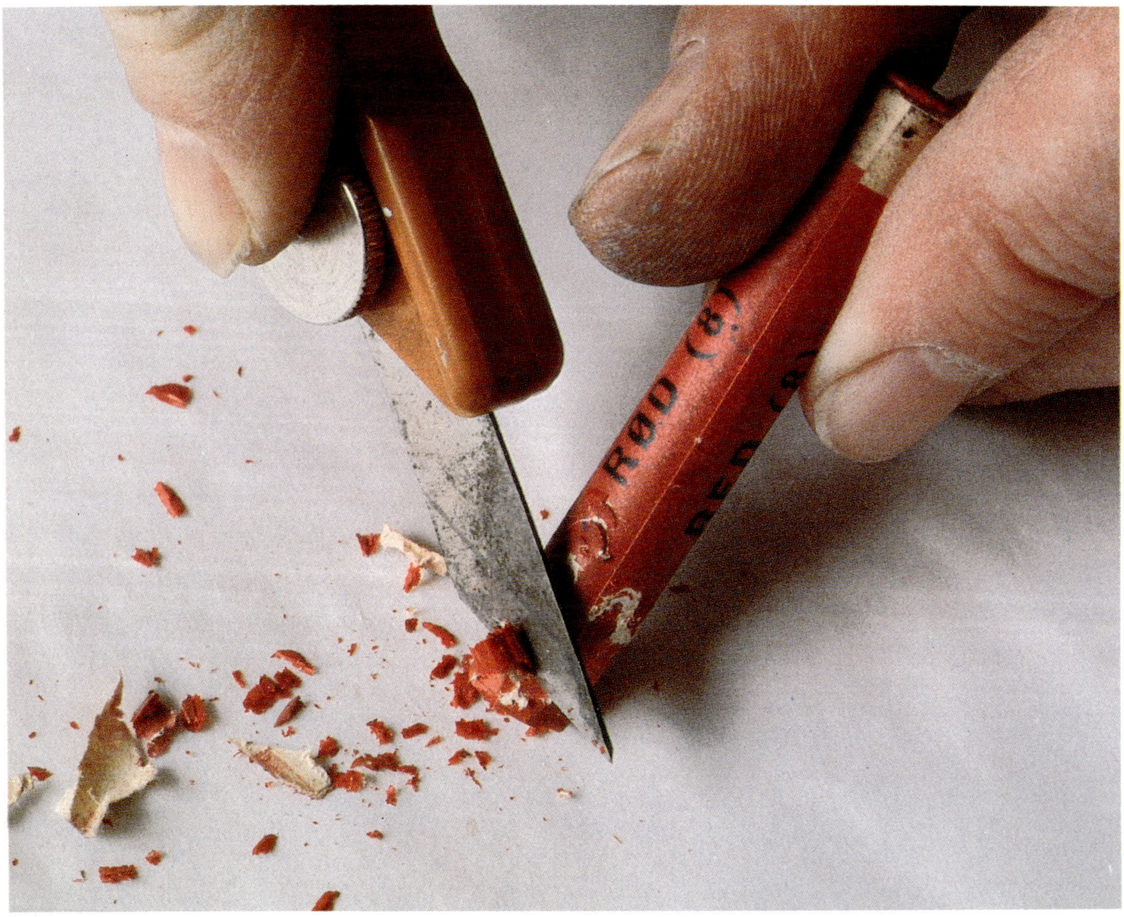

Sharpening pastels. For very fine work, rub the end of the pastel lightly on fine sandpaper to chamfer a point **(above)**. *Oil pastels are more firmly bound and harder than true pastels, so these can be sharpened with a knife* **(left)**. *Sharp pastels are useful for line work but as they are very soft you will have to resharpen them quite often if you are to avoid smudgy, ill-defined lines.*

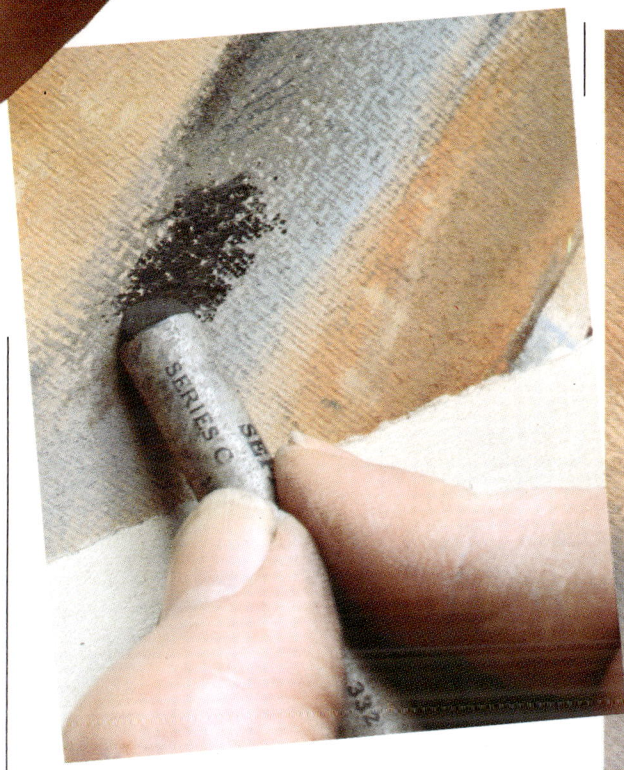

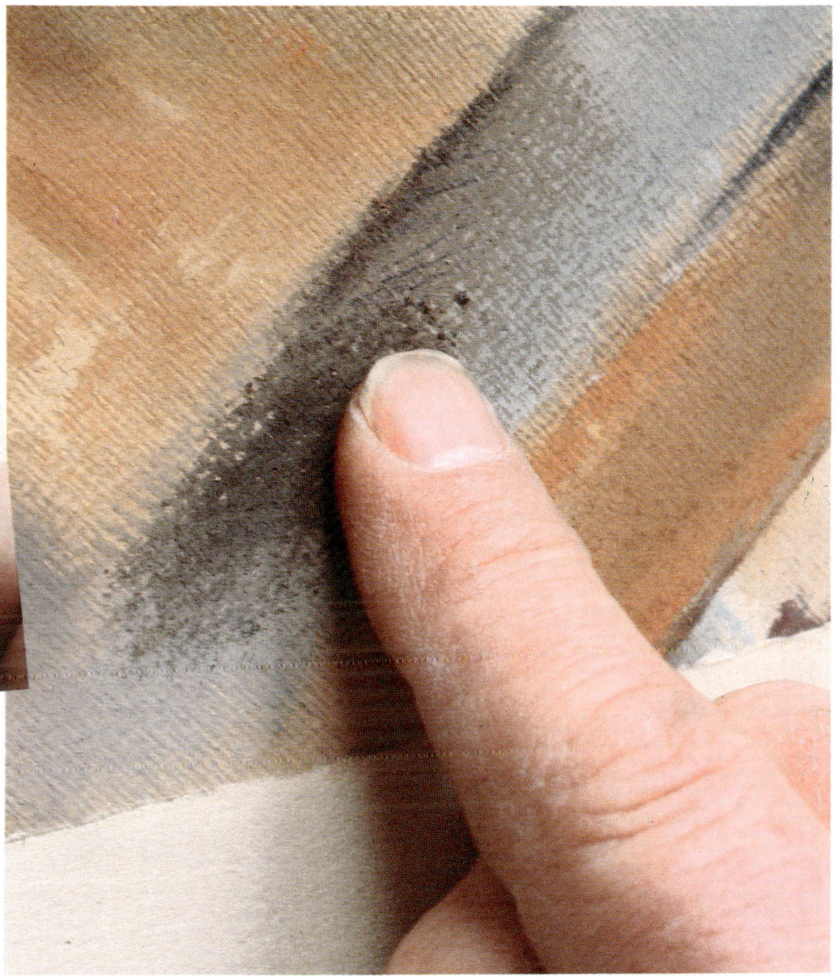

Laying an area of tone. Draw in a small area of thick colour using the blunted end of the pastel **(top)**. *Using your fingertips spread the colour slightly* **(right)** *and work it into the area required. If necessary more colour can be added for extra density. This method can also be used to blend two or more colours. Work with the board tilted slightly so the pastel dust falls off the drawing.*

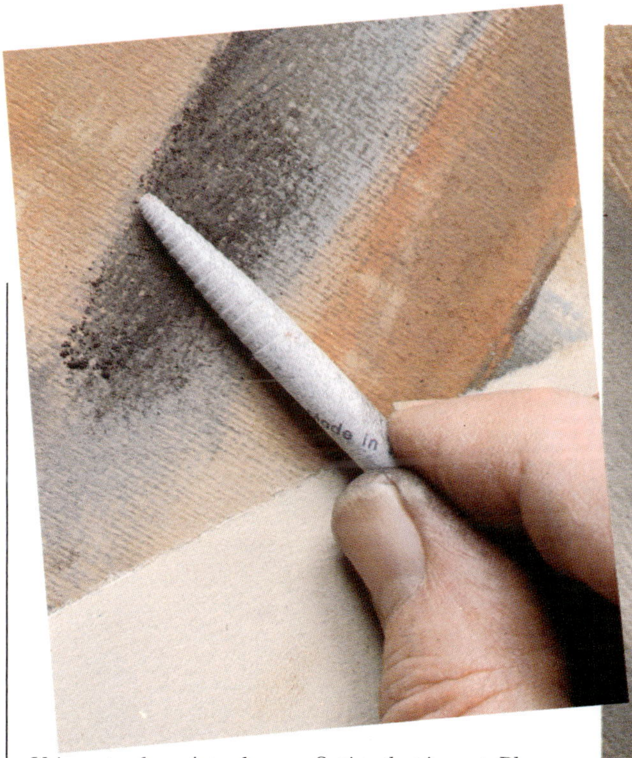

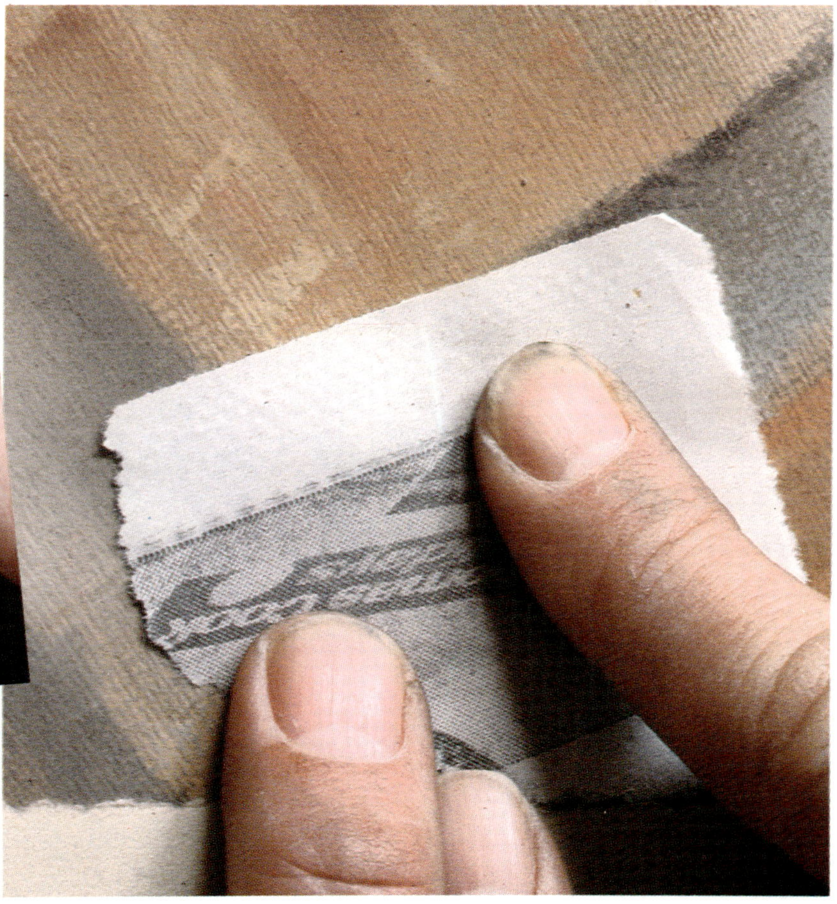

Using a torchon. A torchon is a pencil shaped tool, made from tightly rolled paper, which can be used to spread the pastel. This is useful for fine details **(above)**.

Setting the pigment. Place a piece of newspaper over the area of colour and rub it. This pushes the pastel into the grain of the paper making it less likely to smudge **(right)**.

Using a coloured support. The grainy texture of pastel is well suited to coloured paper which shows through the pigment modifying and unifying the colour. You can mix colours by laying them down as short, open strokes **(below)**. *They mix optically the perceived colour being a product of the brown and blue pastels and the pink support.*

Combining different marks. **Right** *the artist has laid down lightly hatched strokes of colour, and beside that solid colour into which he has worked a lighter tone. It is worth spending time experimenting to see how many different marks you can elicit from a stick of pastel.*

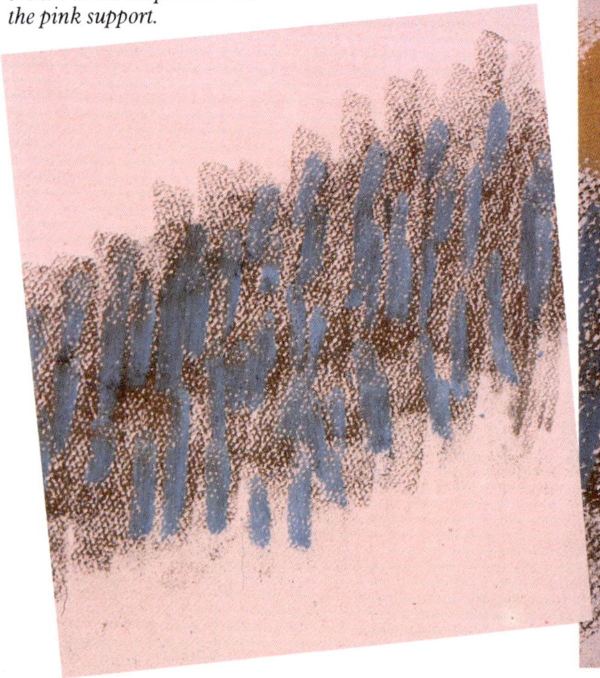

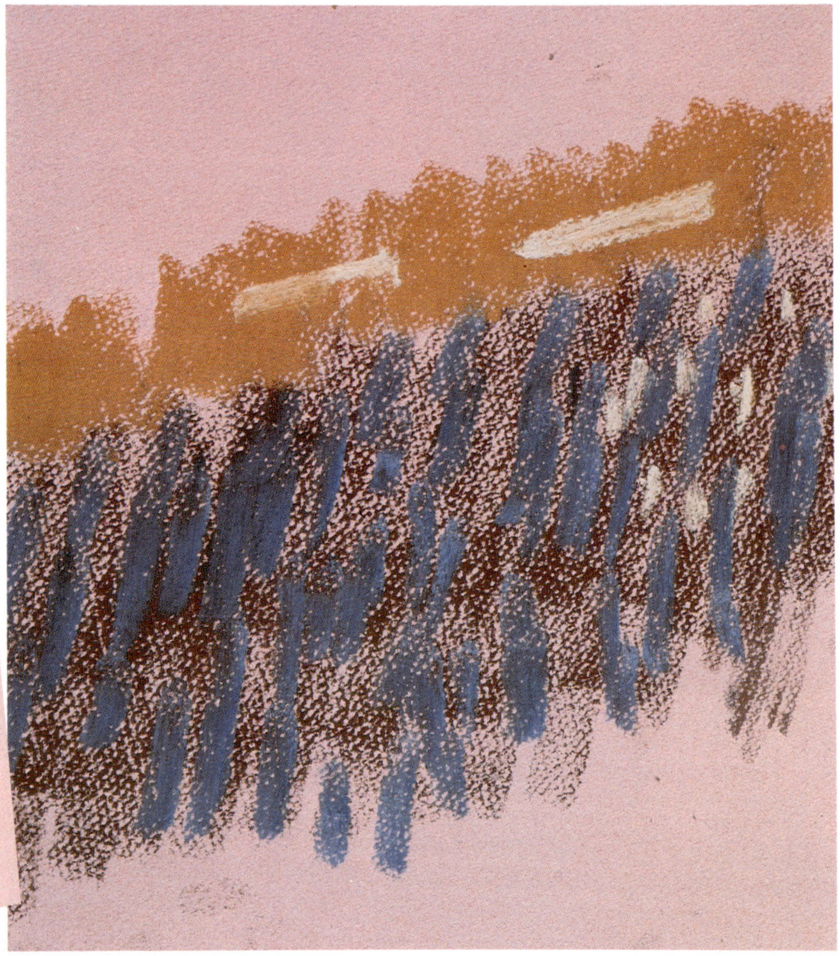

Using charcoal. Strong dark tones can be laid in with charcoal. Put down broad, black lines and spread them out with the fingertips **(below)**. *Highlights can also be worked into the charcoal, but eventually the colours will clog together — so do not overwork the surface* **(right)**. *The clarity and tonal differences in the drawing will soon be lost if it is not fixed immediately after completion. Pastel drawings are very susceptible to smudging, especially when white and dark colours are used in the same picture.*

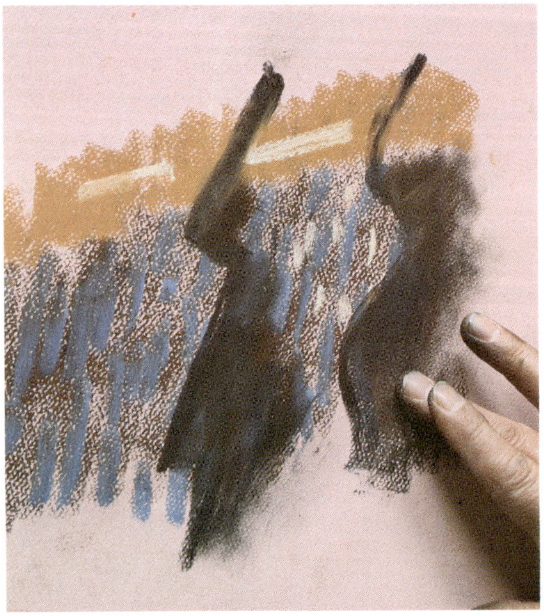

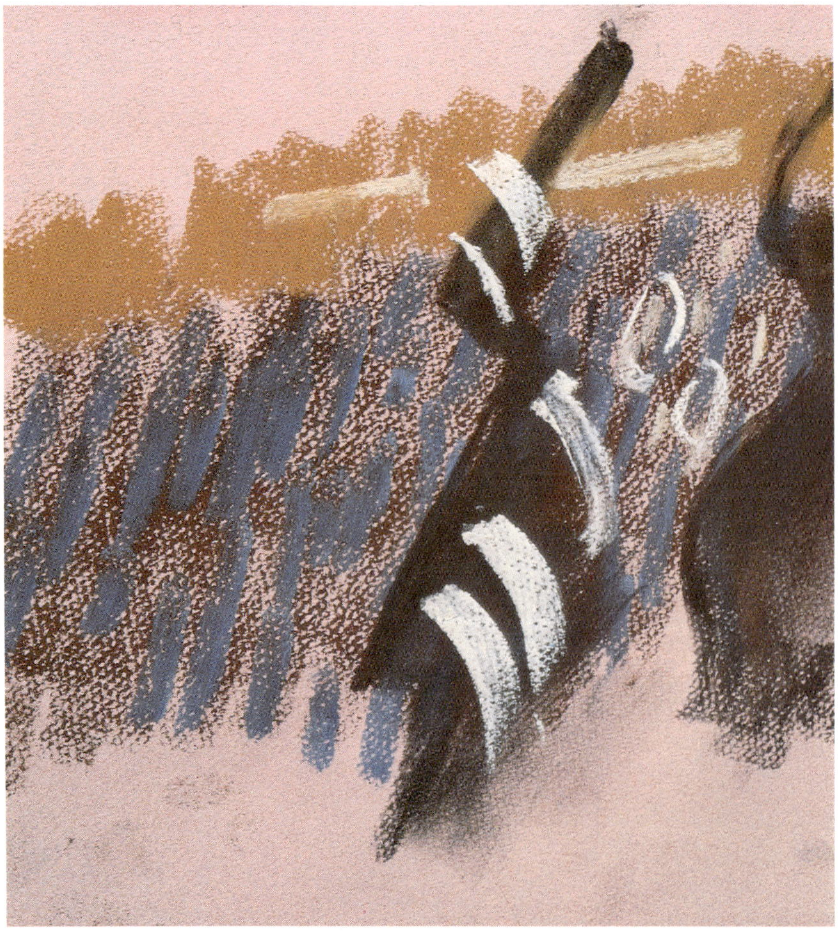

Lifting pastel with a brush. *A soft sable brush can be used to lift excess pastel and to lighten the tone. Blow away surplus dust* **(right)**. Adding detail with charcoal. *For fine work, sharpen the end of the charcoal by rubbing it lightly on sandpaper. Charcoal can be used to add strong, crisp detail. Pastel can be worked over the charcoal* **(below)** *and the hard line can be 'knocked back' by blending. To protect the drawing while you work you should rest your hand on a piece of paper* **(bottom)**. Highlighting with a soft rubber. *Knead the rubber to a point and lift a small area of the pastel to obtain lighter tones* **(bottom right)**

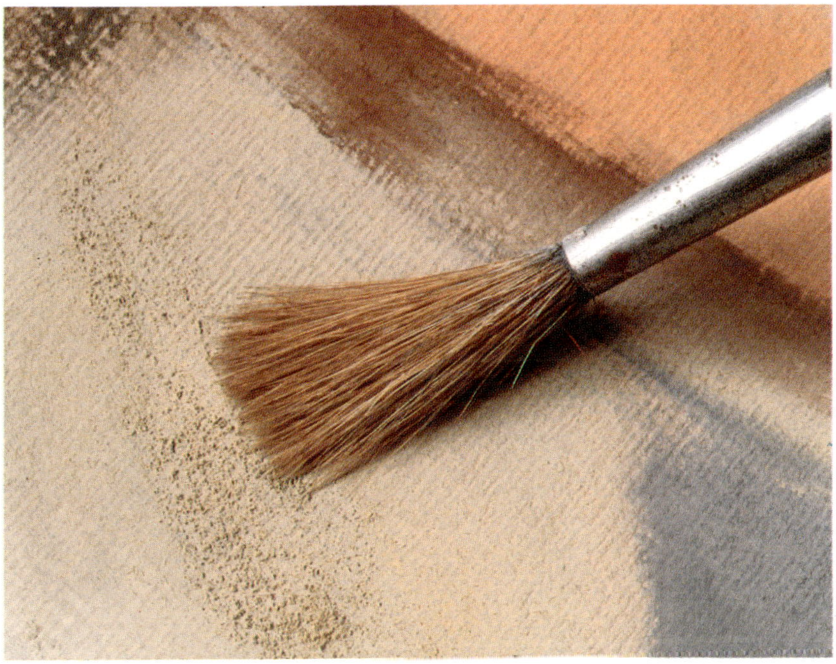

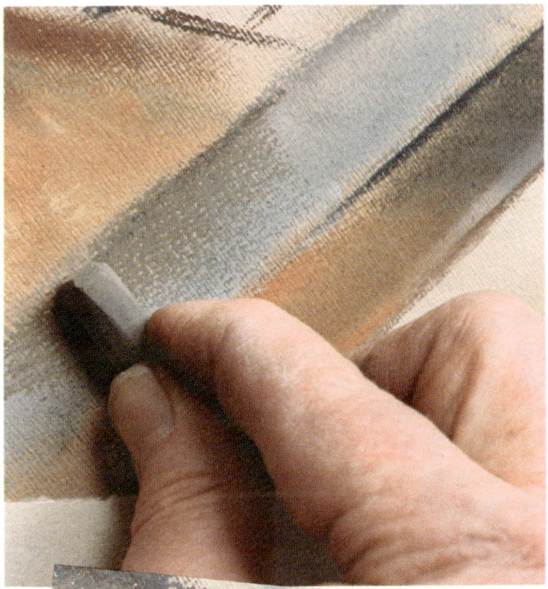

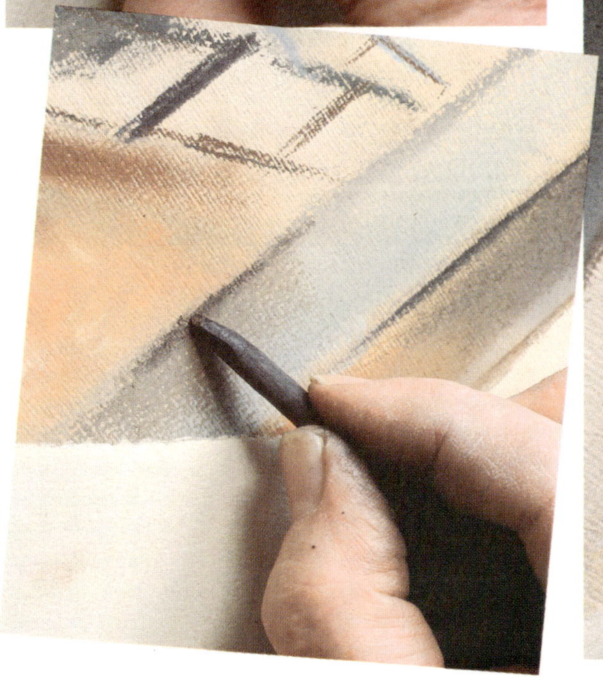

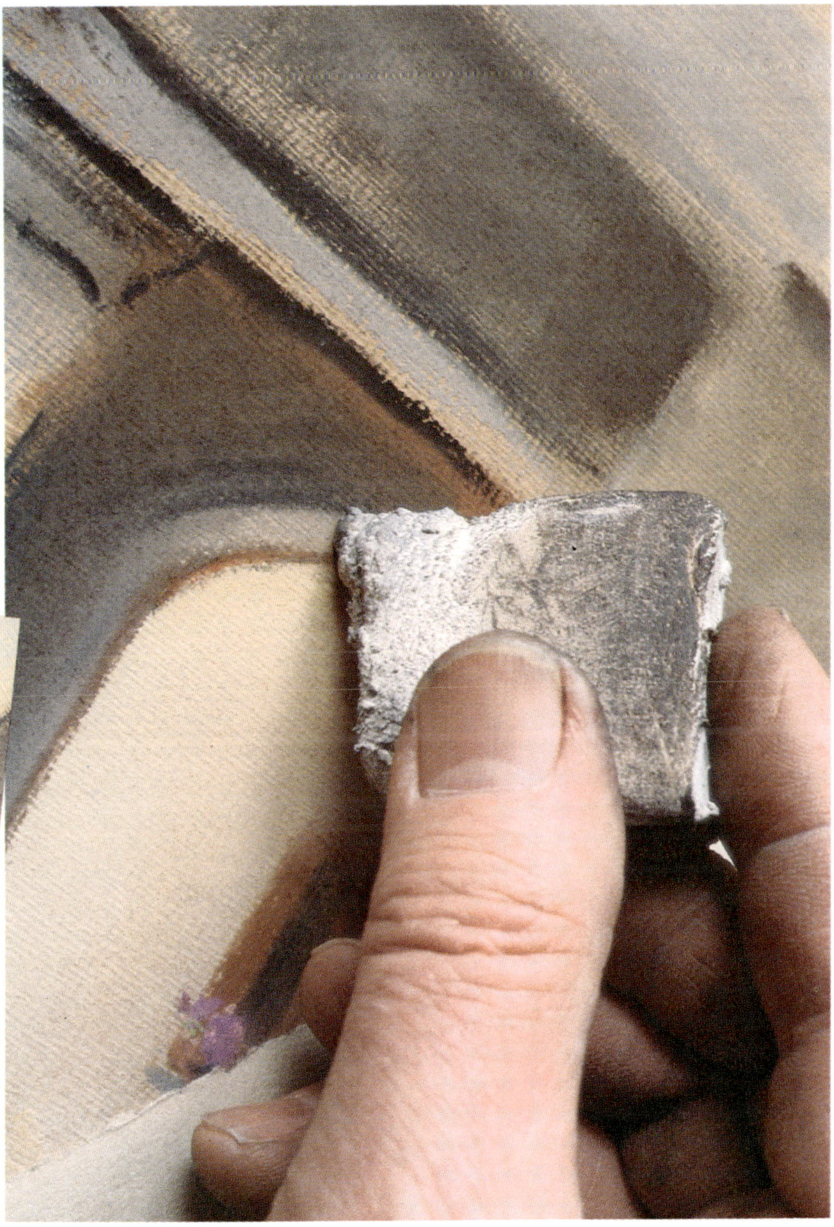

USING COLOUR TO EXPRESS MOOD

Our feelings play an important part in the way we perceive colour and these emotional responses can be used to create particular mood in a drawing or painting.

An artist uses colour for expressive reasons as well as reasons of literal representation — it is yet another means of communicating what he or she feels. What the artist is trying to say and the mood which is being conveyed should be apparent to the viewer through the choice of colours and the way they are used.

On the next pages we show an example of the way in which the atmosphere of a painting can be changed by adjusting the colours. The artist has taken a single subject and treated it in two different ways. He had used pastel because he wanted to develop his ideas as quickly as possible. How do you respond to the two finished pastels?

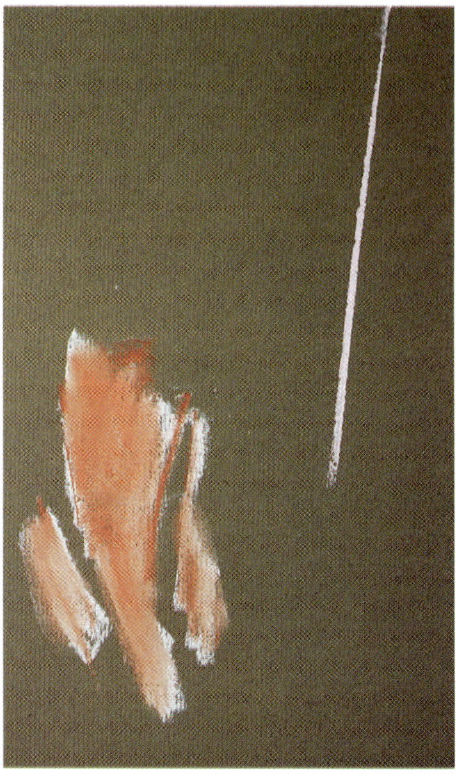

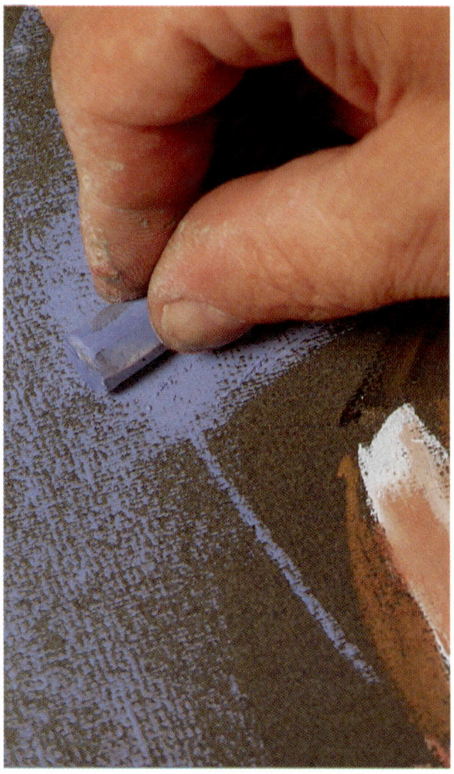

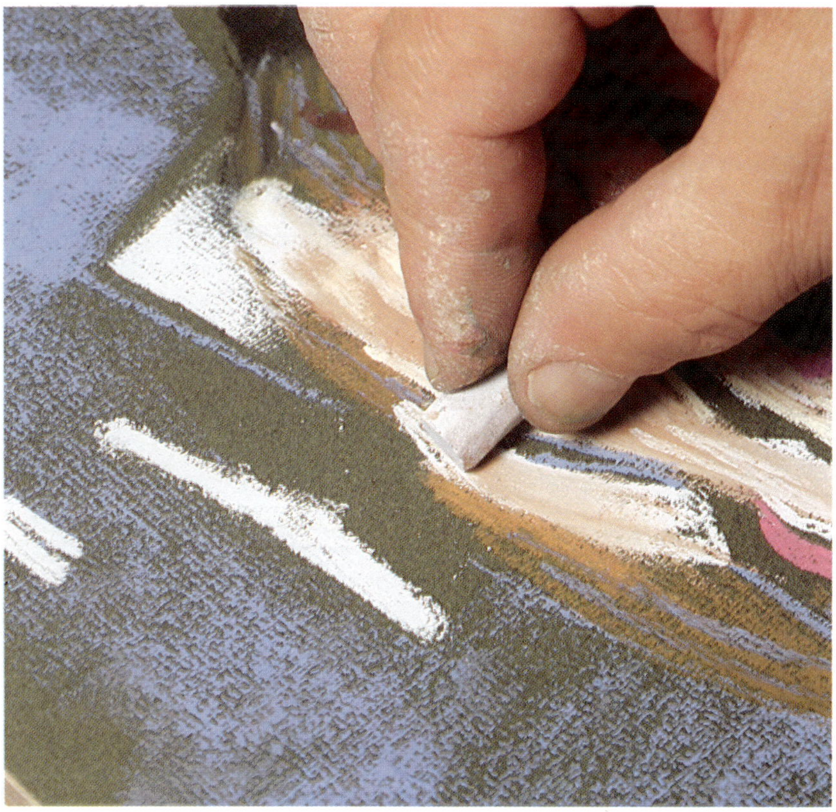

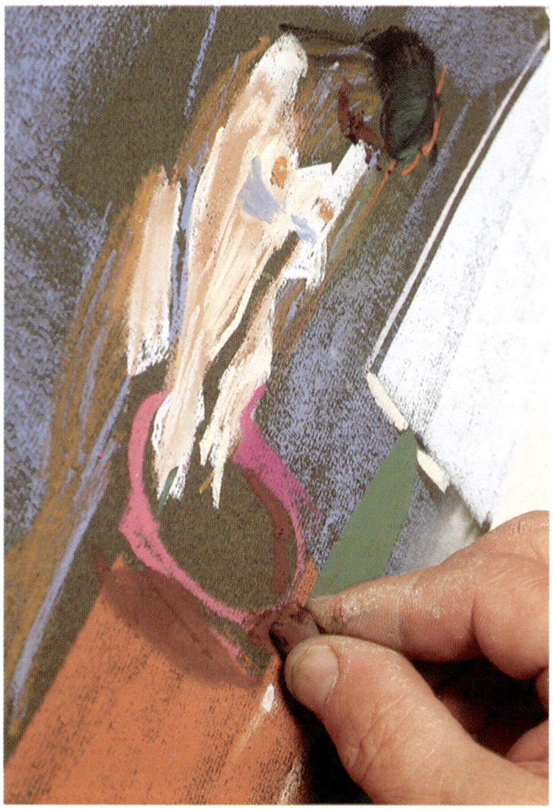

The mood of a picture is usually dictated by the colour and tone. By slightly changing either of these the feeling of a painting can be completely altered. In this exercise the artist makes two pictures of the same subject, using different colours and a different tinted paper for each one.

For the first picture he chose a dark paper. A cool colour, such as olive green, is ideal **(top left)**. *Using a set of general purpose soft pastels, and keeping the colours readily to hand, he starts to block in areas of the composition.*

When doing such an exercise do not be too self-conscious about choosing suitable colours, but try to maintain a fairly rich tone in the picture. The artist blocks in the background in a strong blue or mauve, **(top right)**. *The artist applies the colour using the side of the stick so that the colour builds up quickly. This will later be echoed throughout the composition. He develops the figure, pressing hard on the pastels where a particularly dense tone is required* **(above left)**. *He keeps the areas of colour quite simple and separate, without blending and mixing the colours.*

The artist introduces some deep, bright colours into the pastel drawing **(above right)**. *Deep reds, pinks and oranges all contribute to the overall richness of the colour theme. Some of the tinted paper is allowed to show through between the pastels.*

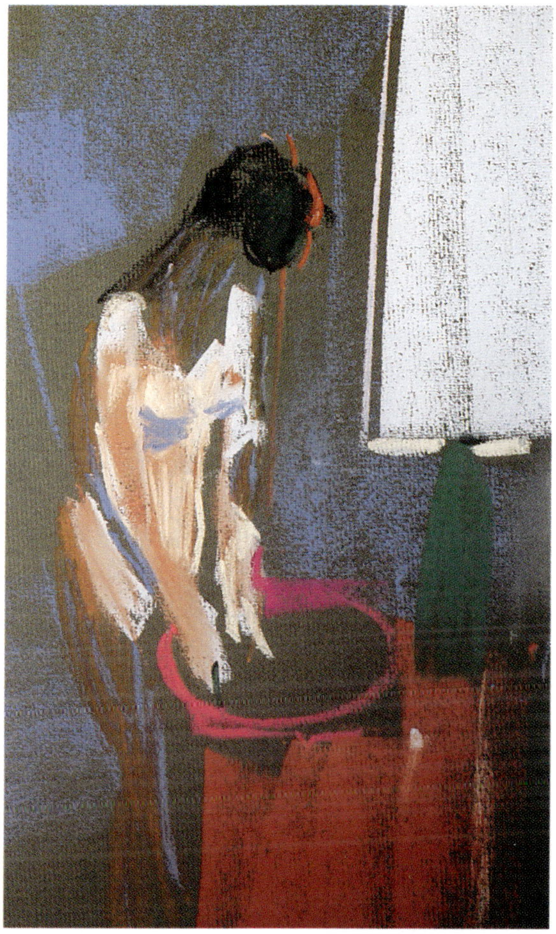

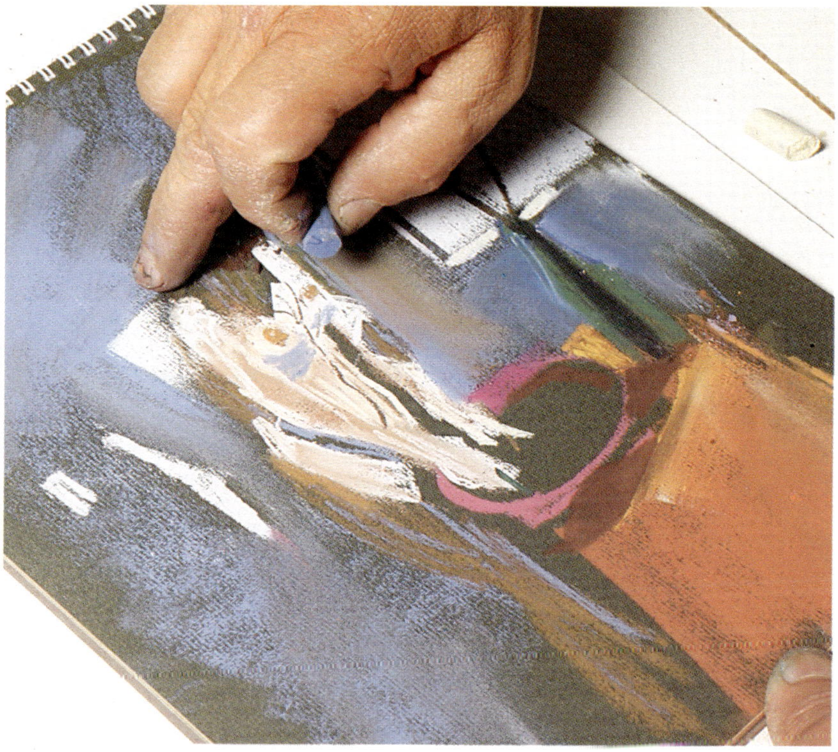

The artist lays in the shadows choosing darker tones **(above)**. *The overall composition should work as a design, so he develops the whole picture instead of concentrating on particular areas, balancing attention to the graphic qualities and negative shapes in the drawing. He rubs the background colour to get a more solid effect* **(top right)** *taking the background colour into the figure* **(below)** *and keeping the drawing simple and the shapes general. He adds details such as the flowers* **(right)** *and works into the shapes with darker tones to give form and depth.*

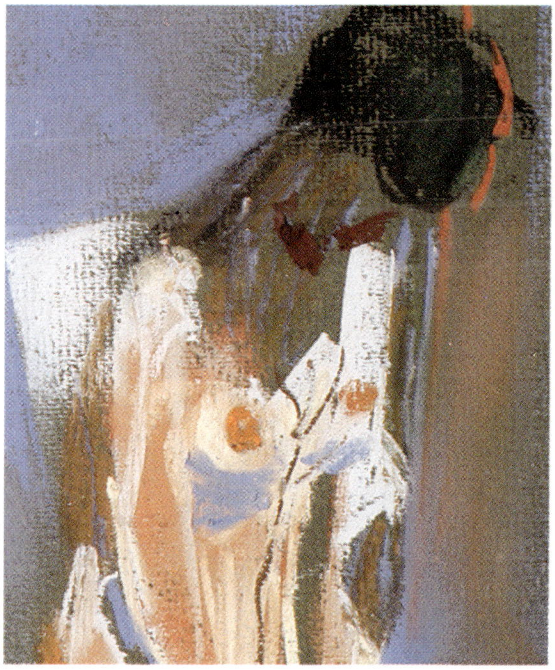

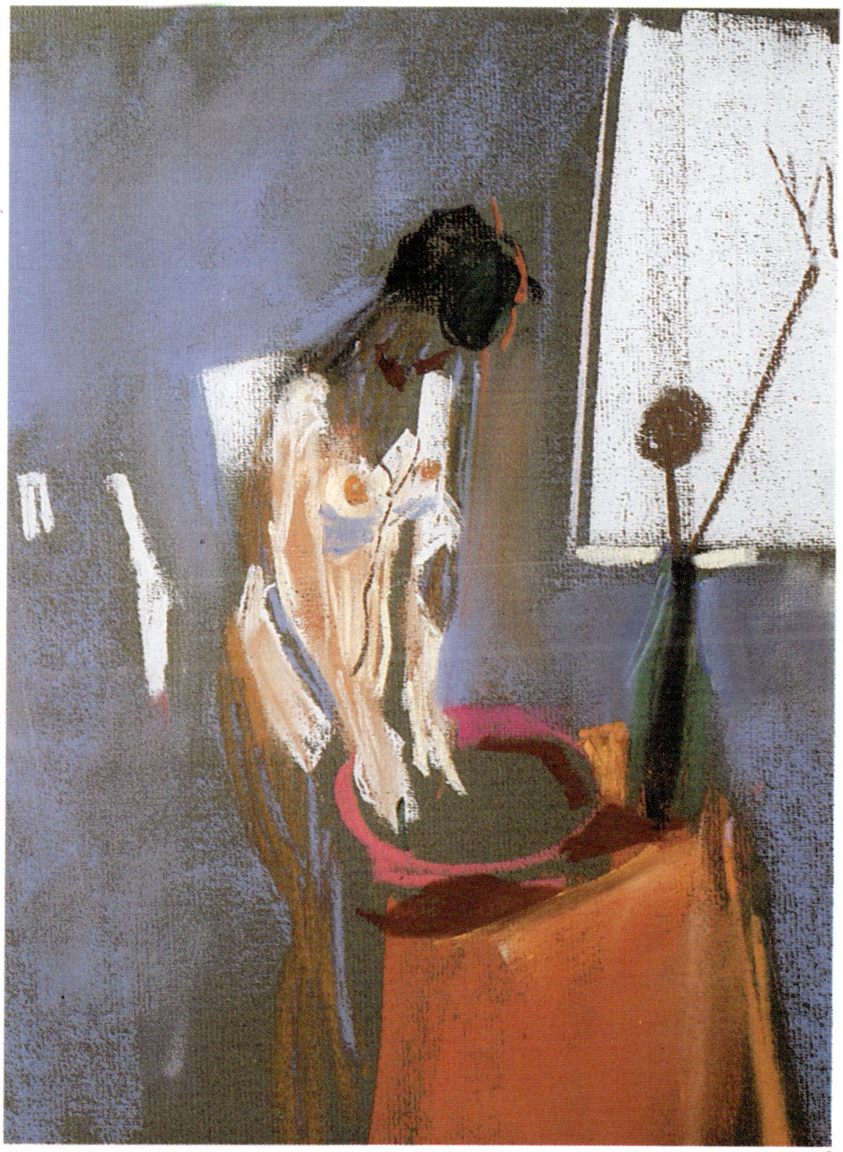

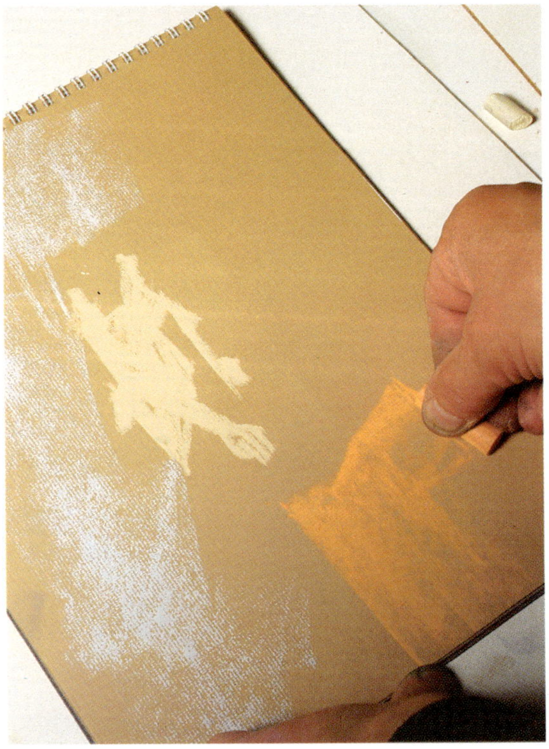

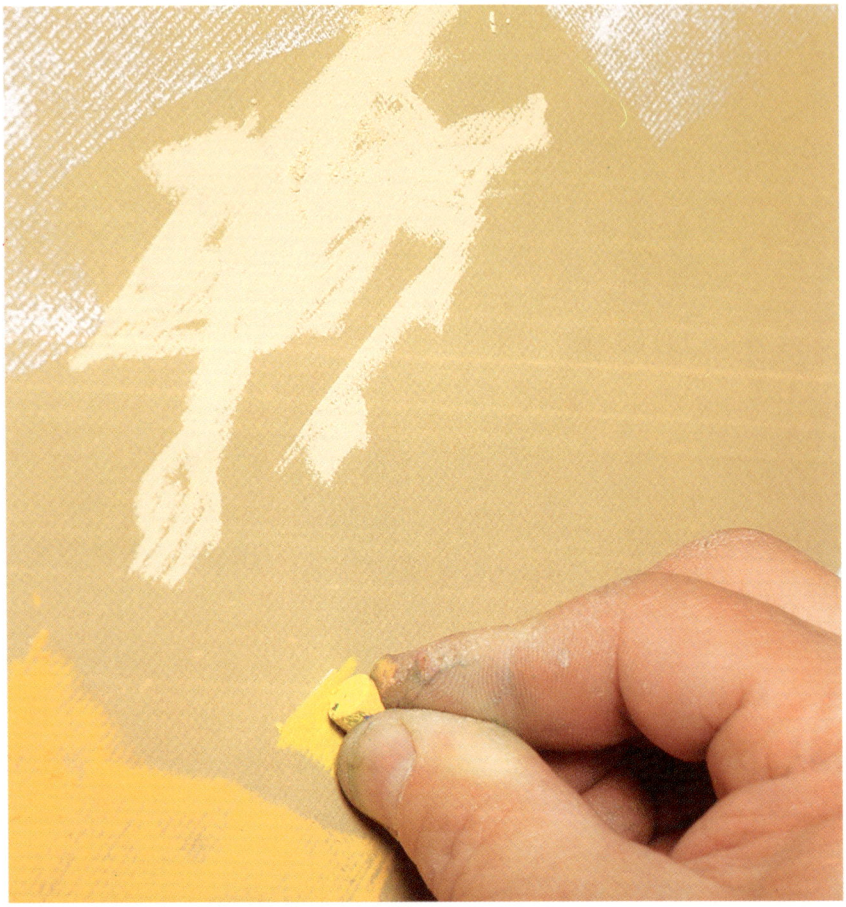

For the second picture the artist takes exactly the same composition — using the first drawing as a reference. Working in the same way as before he begins to block in the light tones **(above)**. *He uses a light, warm tinted paper, and chooses light, warm colours for the intial drawing* **(right and bottom)**.

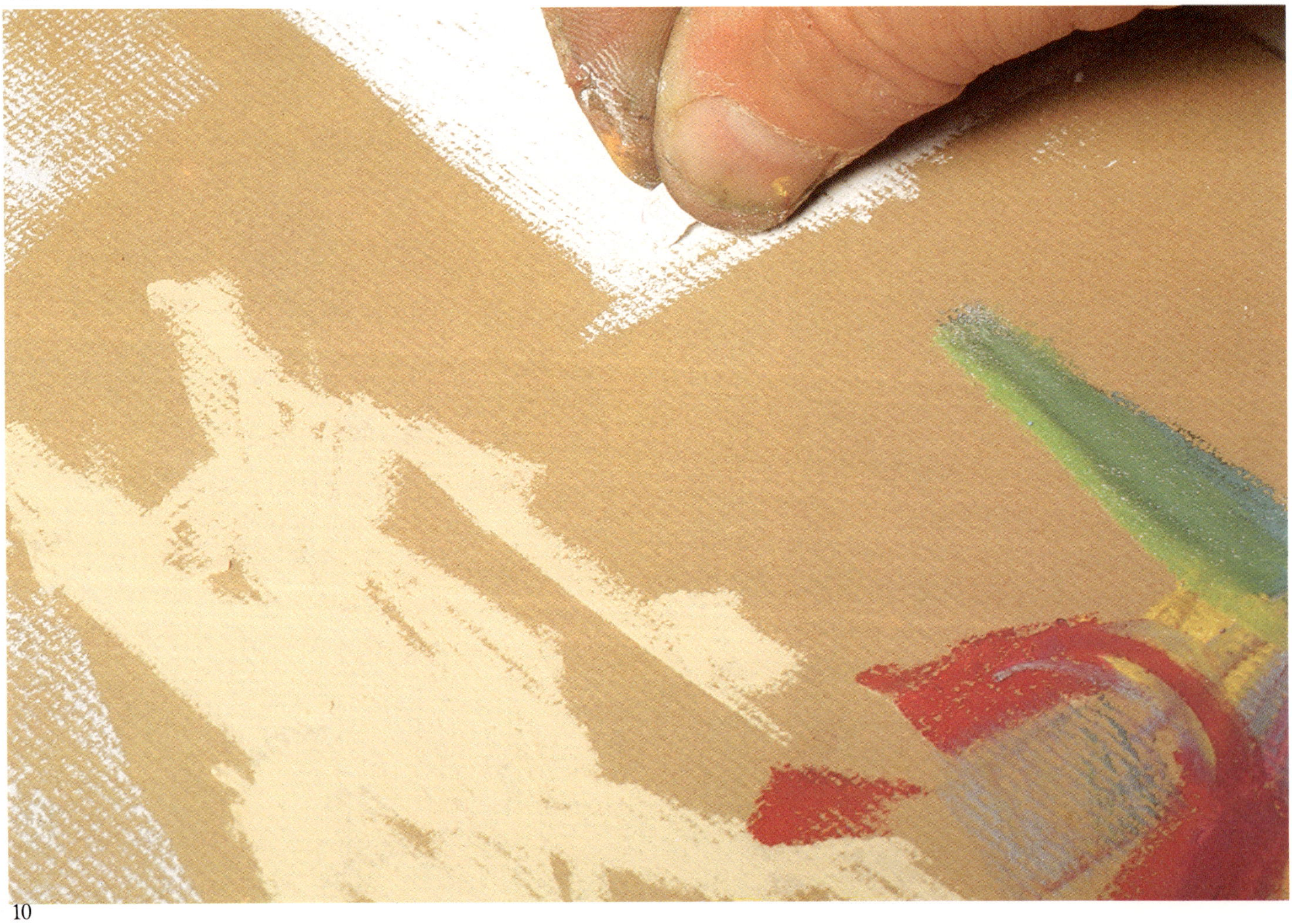

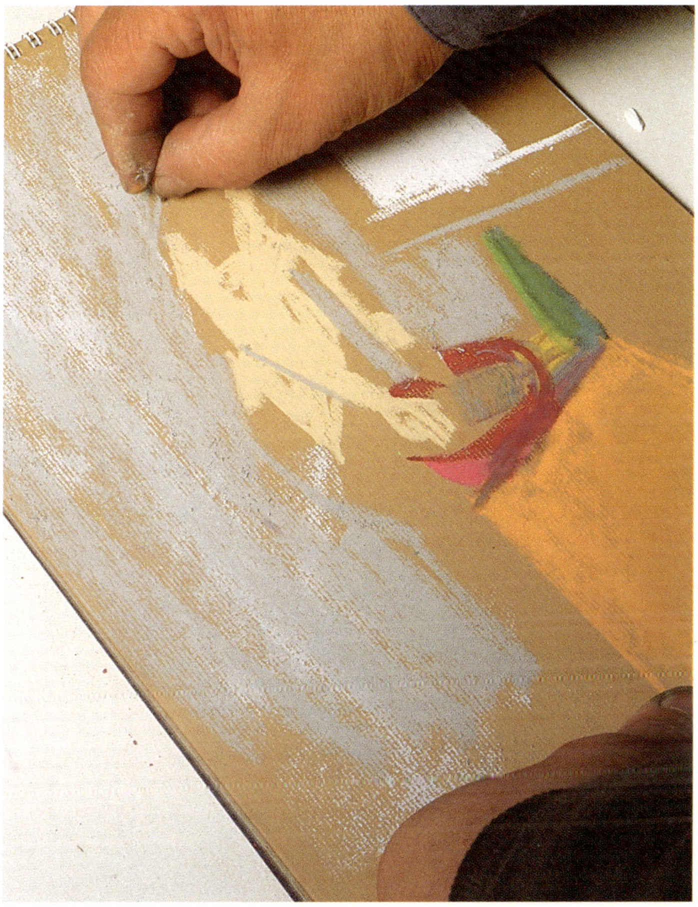

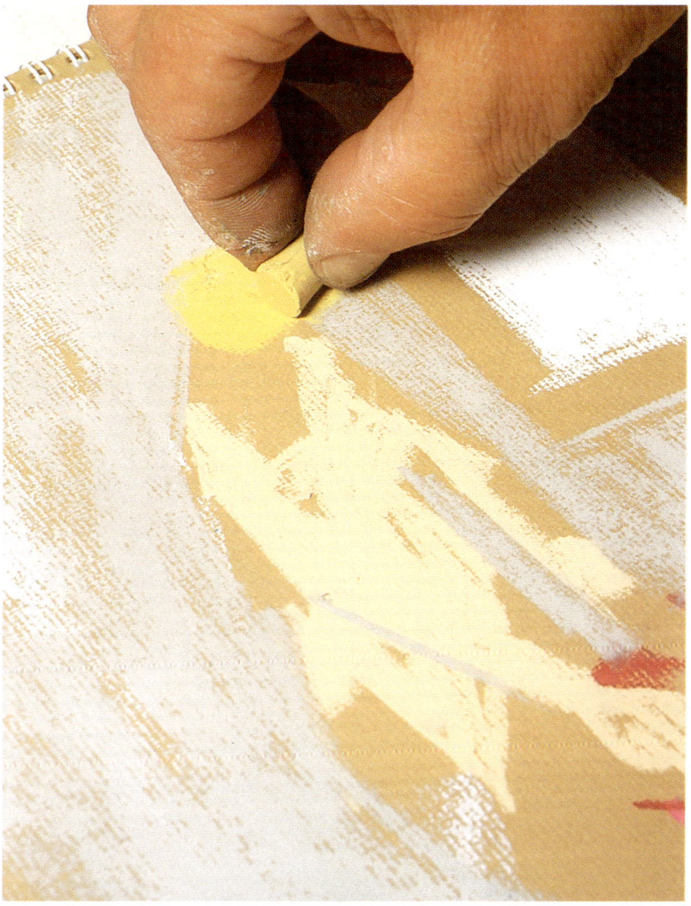

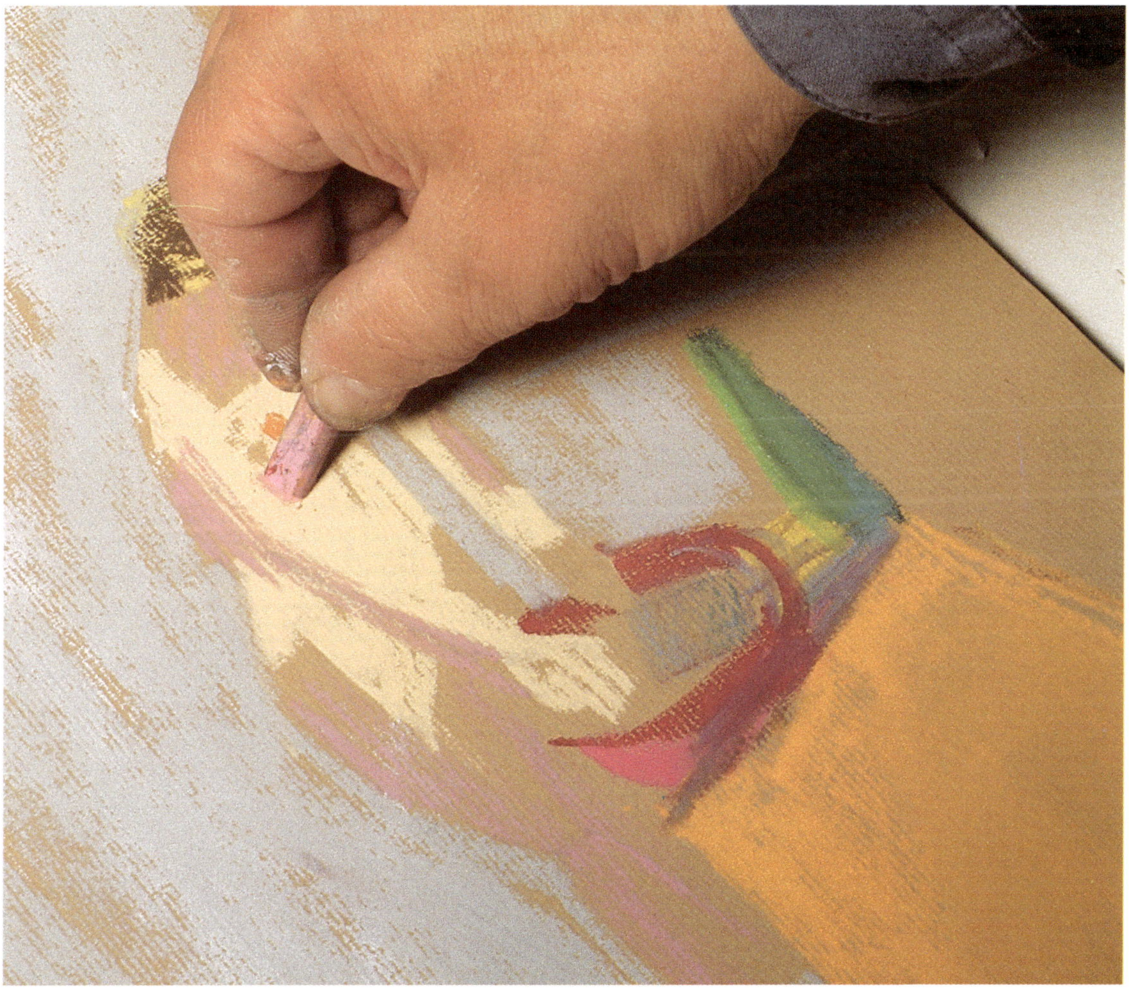

The artist keeps the colours in this picture slightly more subdued than in the first, without making them radically different. For instance he uses a neutral, light grey for the background **(top left)**. *By using lighter local colours he changes the atmosphere* **(top right)**, *working into the figure in warm, pale flesh tones* **(bottom)**.

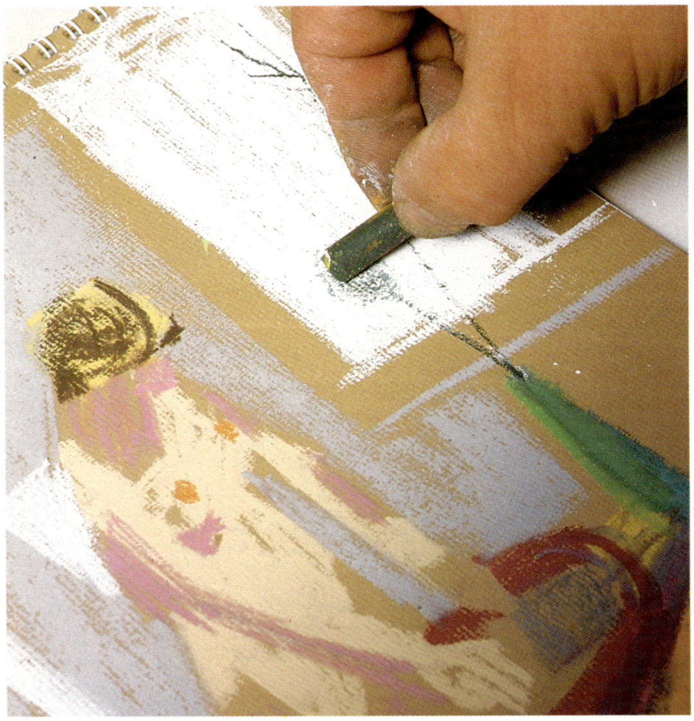

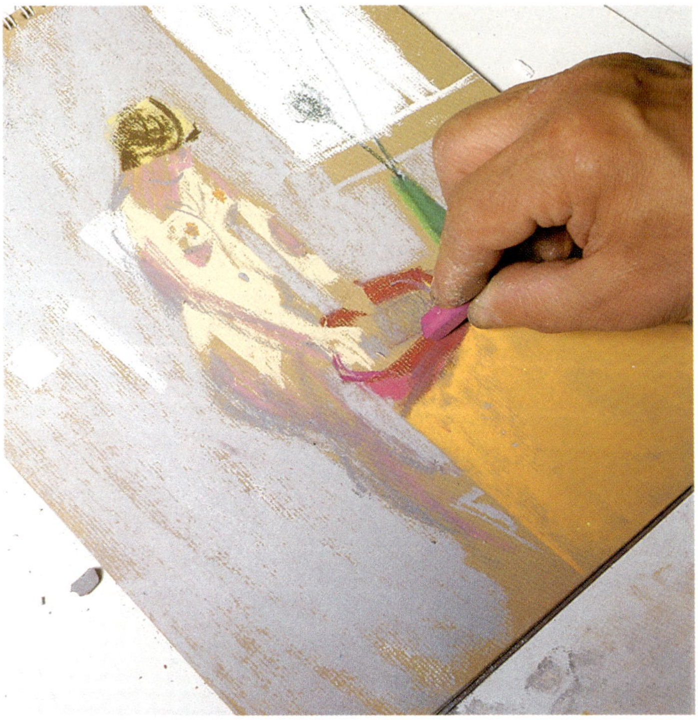

The artist adds details, making the flowers softer and less stark than they were in the earlier picture **(top left)**. *Working into the drawing he adds shadows and dark tones in subdued, muted colours* **(top right)** *to complete the picture* **(bottom right)**.

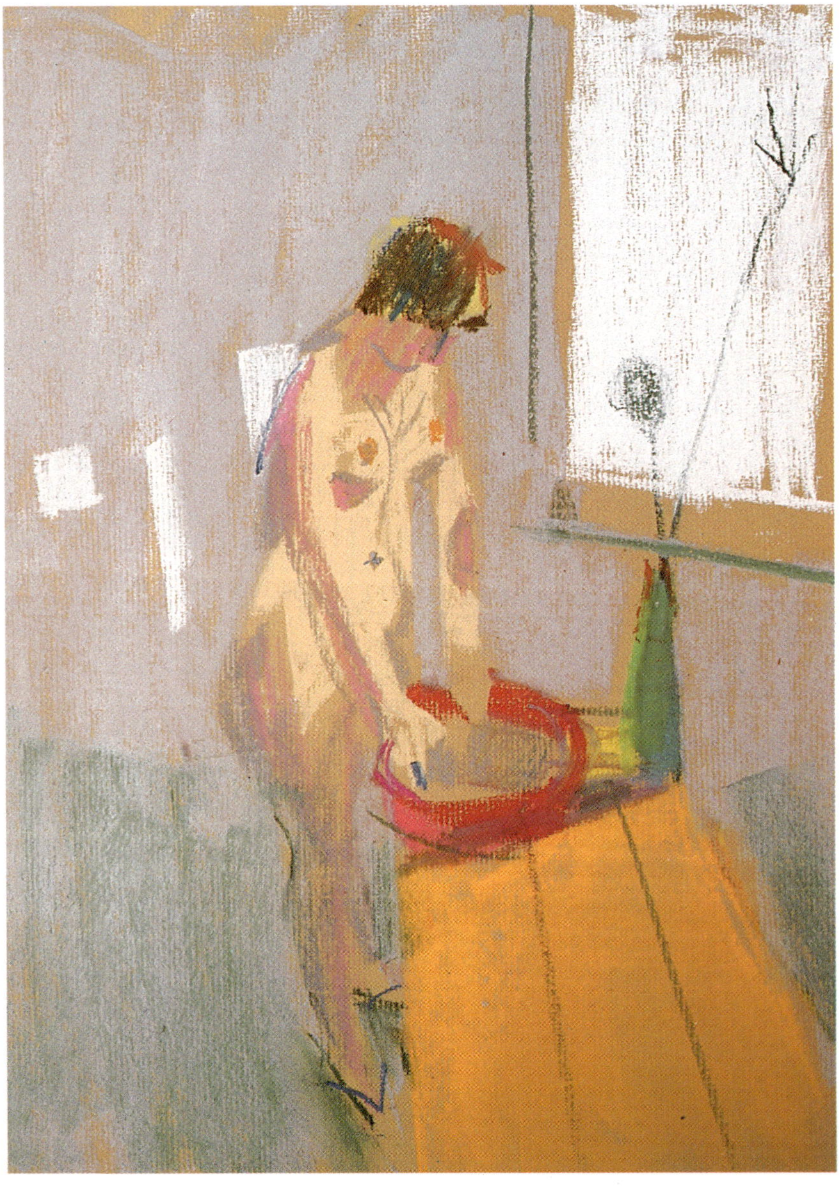

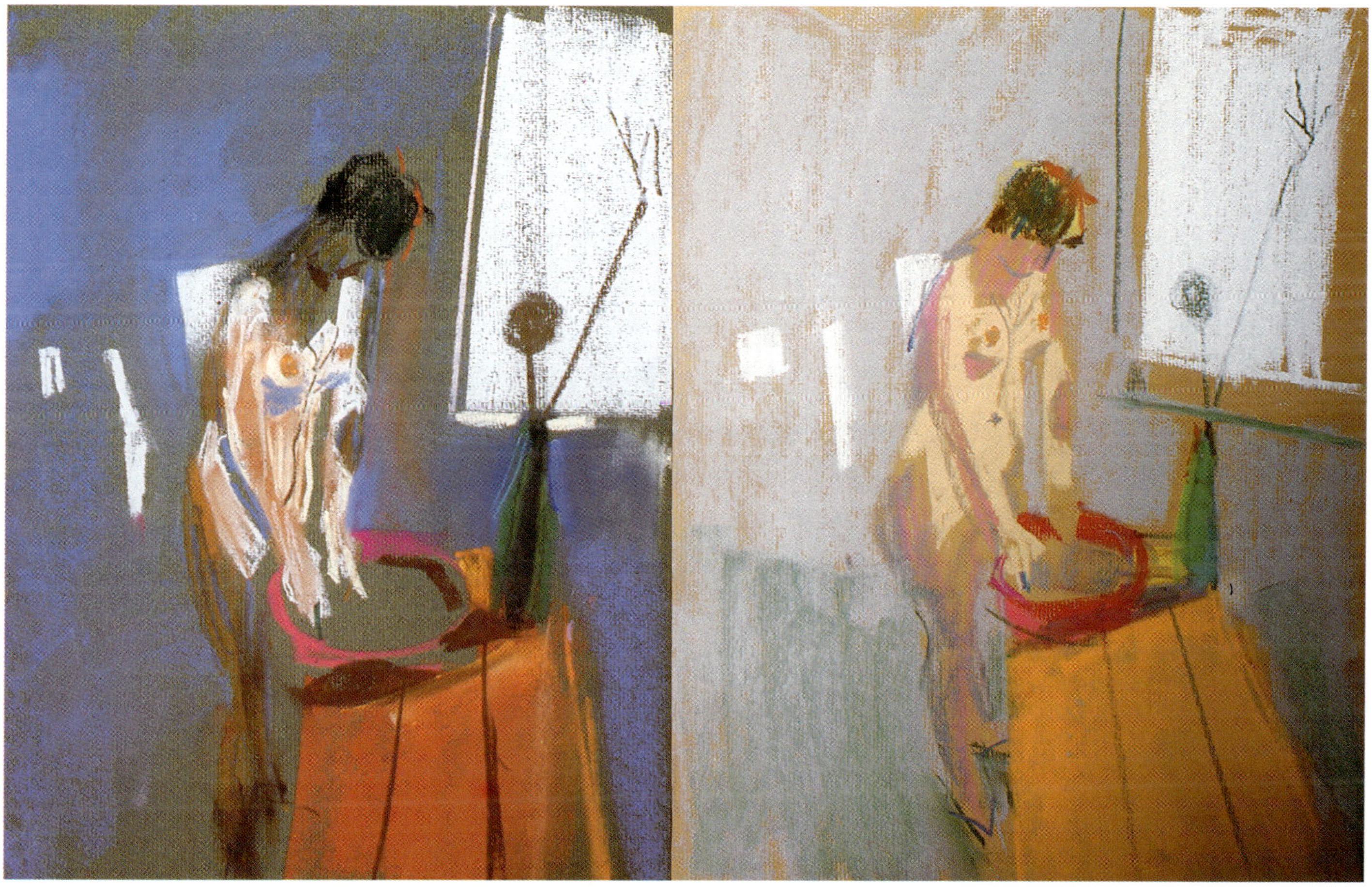

Compare the two finished pictures **(above)**. *Neither drawing is done with a particular colour theme, but each is entirely different in mood and feeling. The heavy, dusky atmosphere of the first picture* **(left)** *is set by the dark paper and rich, deep colours; in the other, the mood is set by the pale paper and light warm colours.*

MATCHES — AN UNUSUAL SUBJECT

For this exercise the artist has taken a small and commonplace object and made it the basis of a painting. The subject is familiar, yet unfamiliar. It is unlikely that you have ever paid more than passing attention to a match. It is useful to try exercises like this every now and then, for the subject, though familiar, is new and fresh and you will be forced to concentrate in order to draw and paint it. It is an excellent way of improving your powers of perception.

A match is very small so there will not be sufficient information for you to become distracted by details. Look for shapes, planes and areas of colour. The painting process will inevitably become a process of abstraction for as the image is enlarged it will begin to break down.

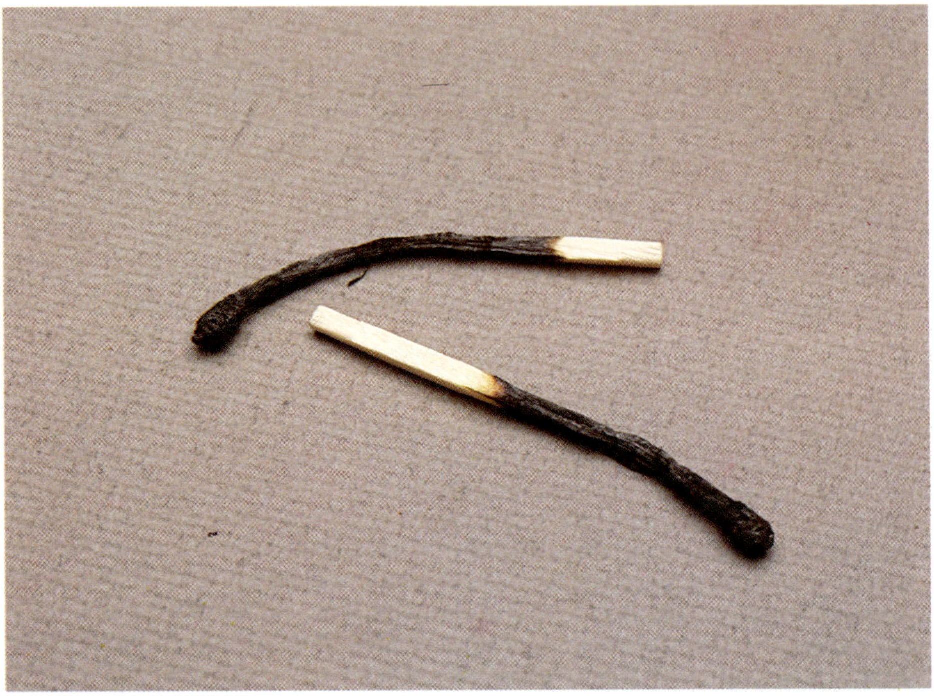

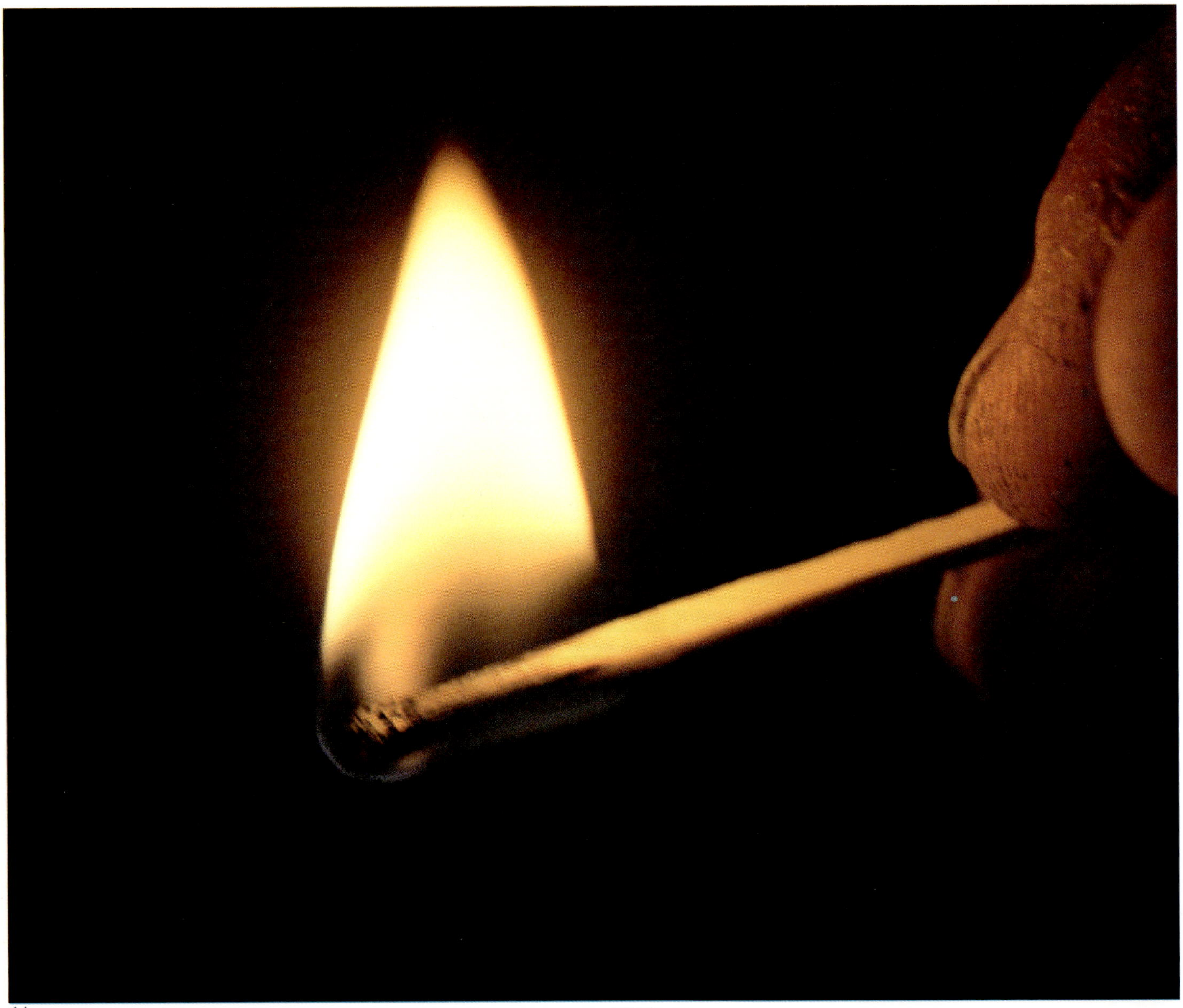

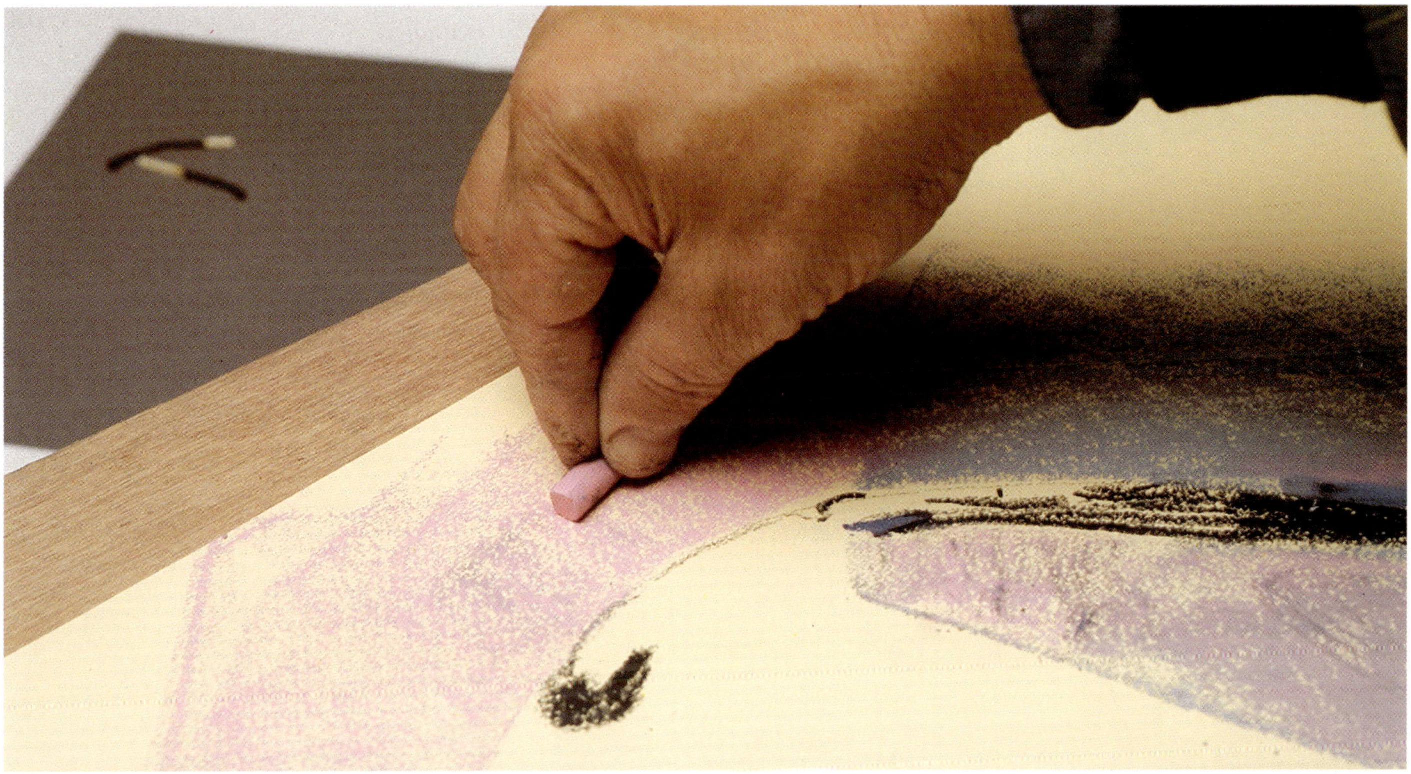

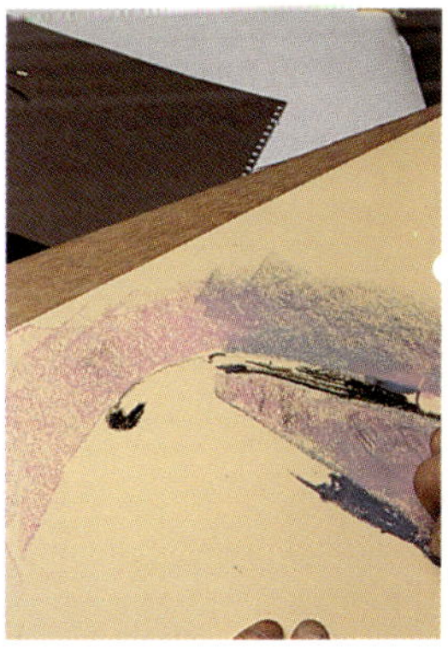

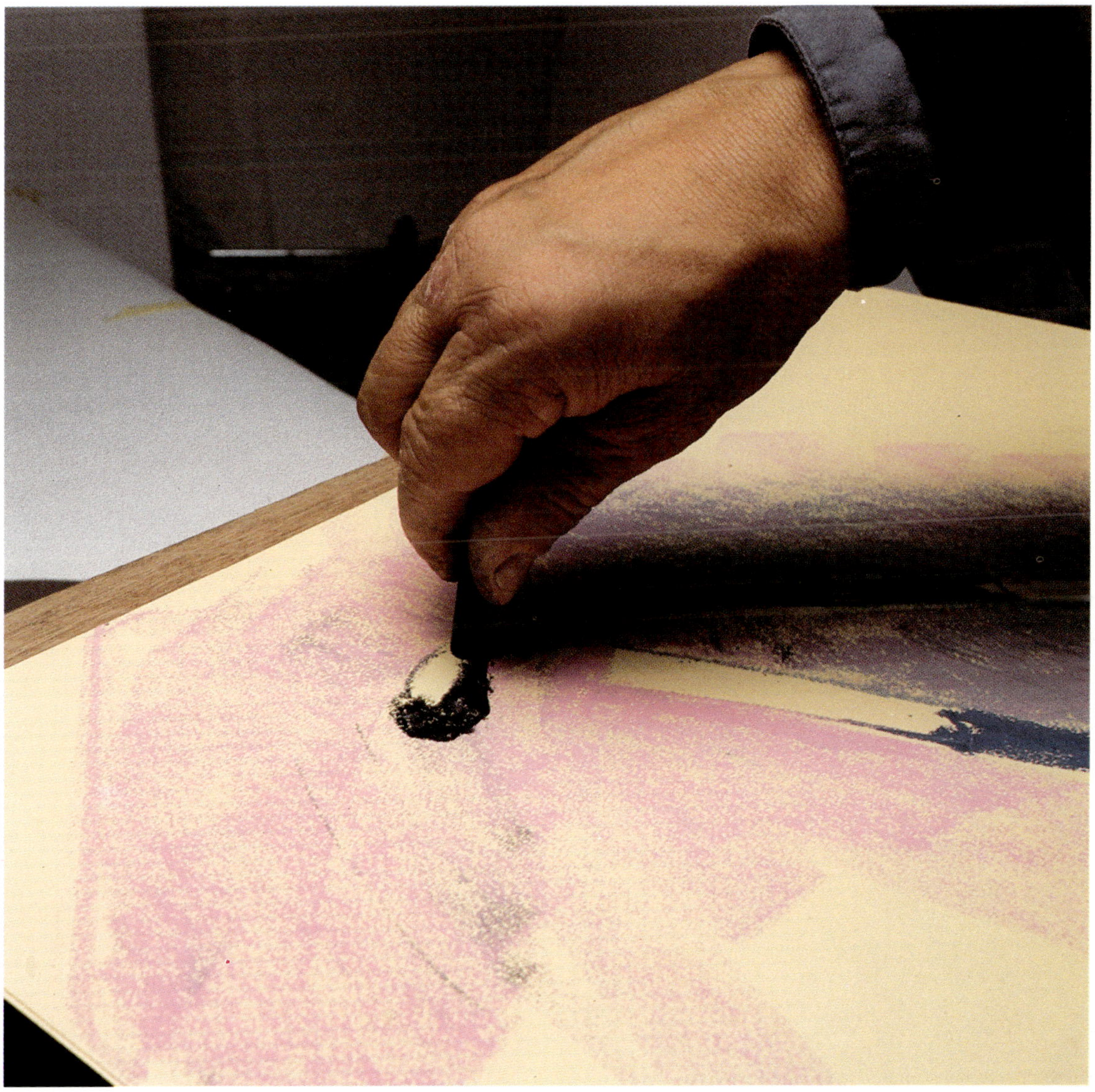

Painting from very small objects entails looking closely at shapes and colours and translating these into a much larger image. The burnt matches **(opposite)** *are a very common 'found object'. The artist put the matches where he could see them easily and sketched them roughly in charcoal. He exaggerated the colours so that they make an impact in the enlarged drawing and uses the background to give him the negative shapes of the subject.*

He uses several closely related colours in the background **(top)**, *blending them to establish an approxmate tone to work on* **(above)**. *Keeping the drawing strong and the image clear, he presses hard on the pastels to produce dense, positive colours* **(right)**.

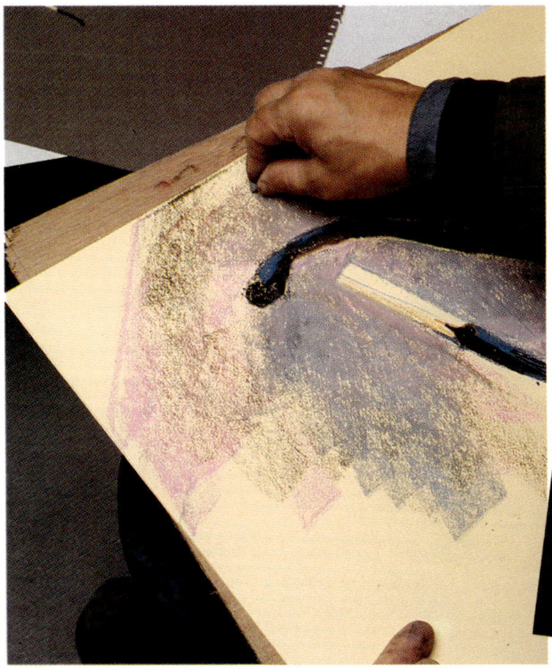

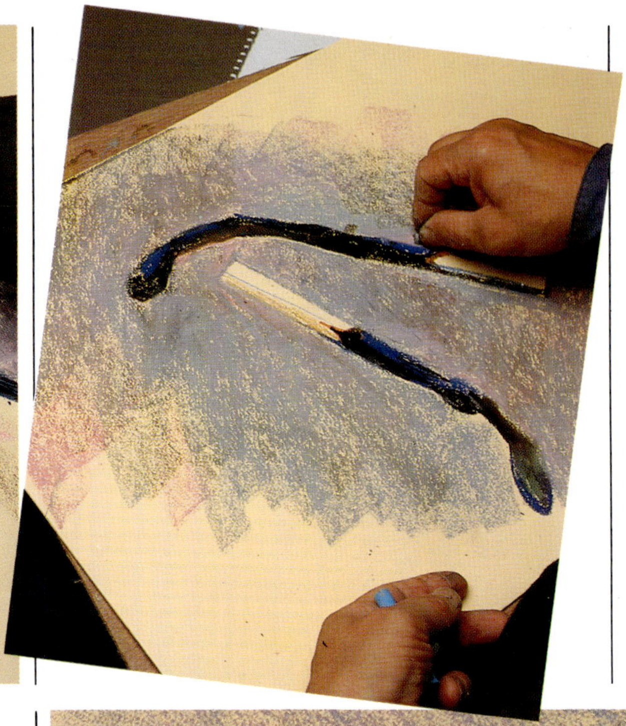

He continues to introduce new colours to increase the richness of the composition. He does not attempt to achieve a realistic effect, but uses the pastels to make a vibrant, interesting picture . He uses a black pastel to intensify the black of the charred part of the match **(bottom left)** *and a brown outline to emphasize the shaded side of the unburnt wood* **(below)**. *The finished picture* **(opposite)** *demonstrates the way in which an everyday object can be used to create an unusual image.*

He continues to build up the colours and tones of the match sticks, using large blocks of colour and bold strokes. He works into the background tones so that they relate to the rest of the picture. He uses the sides of the pastel sticks to cover wide areas **(above)** *working quickly in smooth, broad strokes. Make the background colours denser around the objects to give a feeling of solidity to the arrangement* **(top right)**.

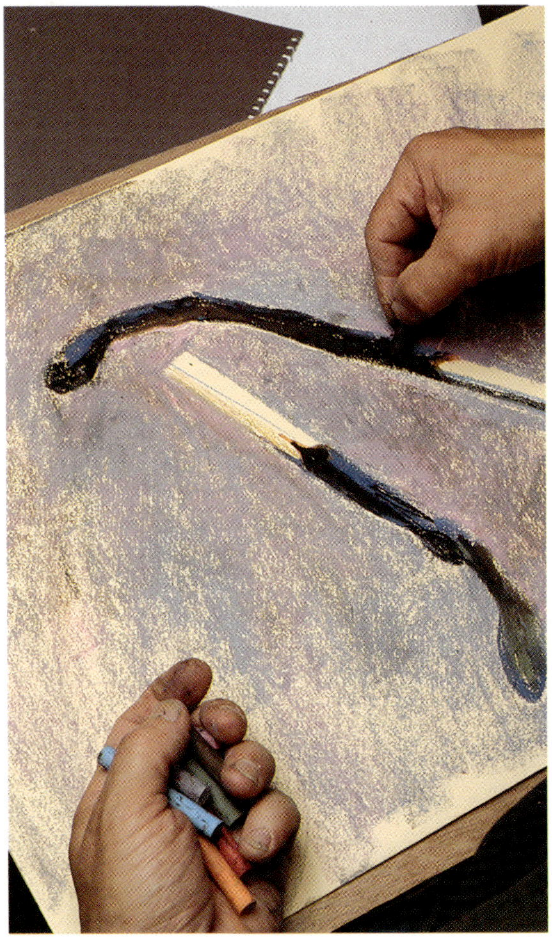

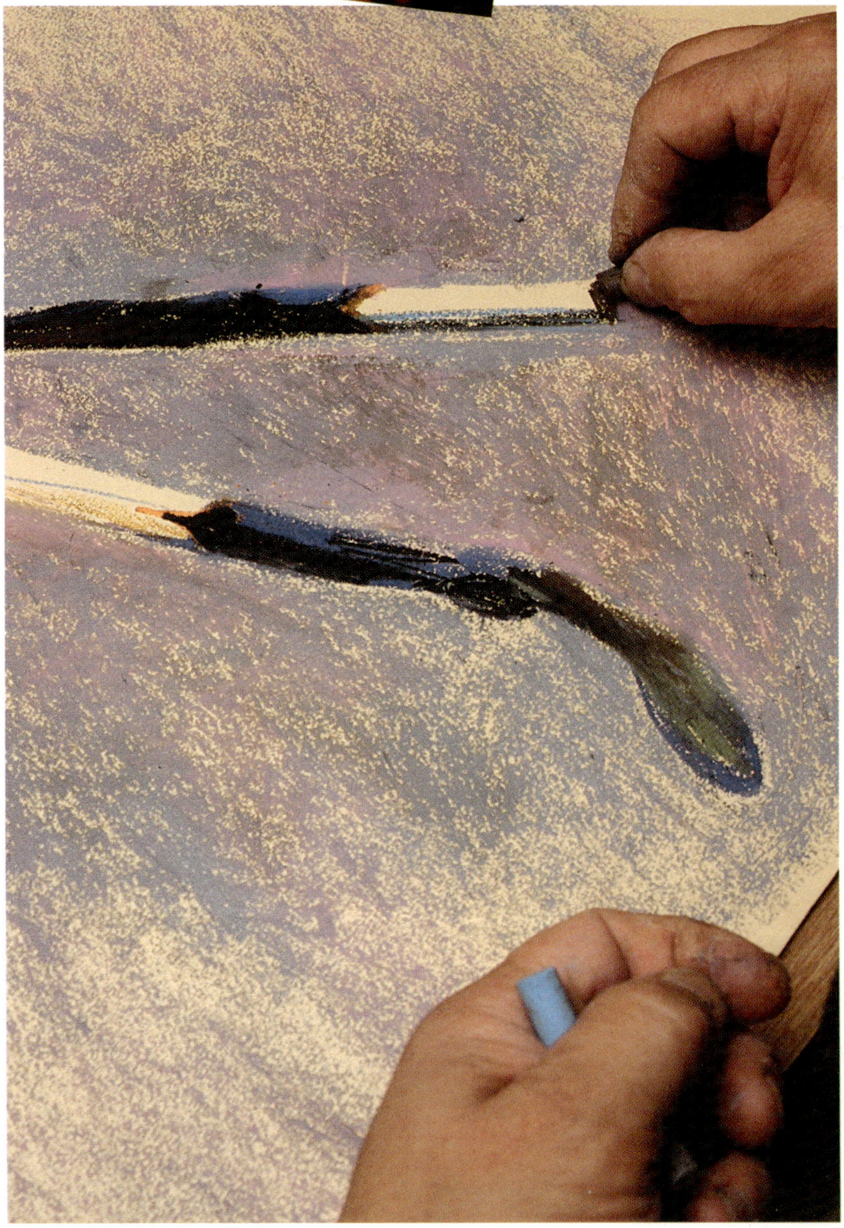

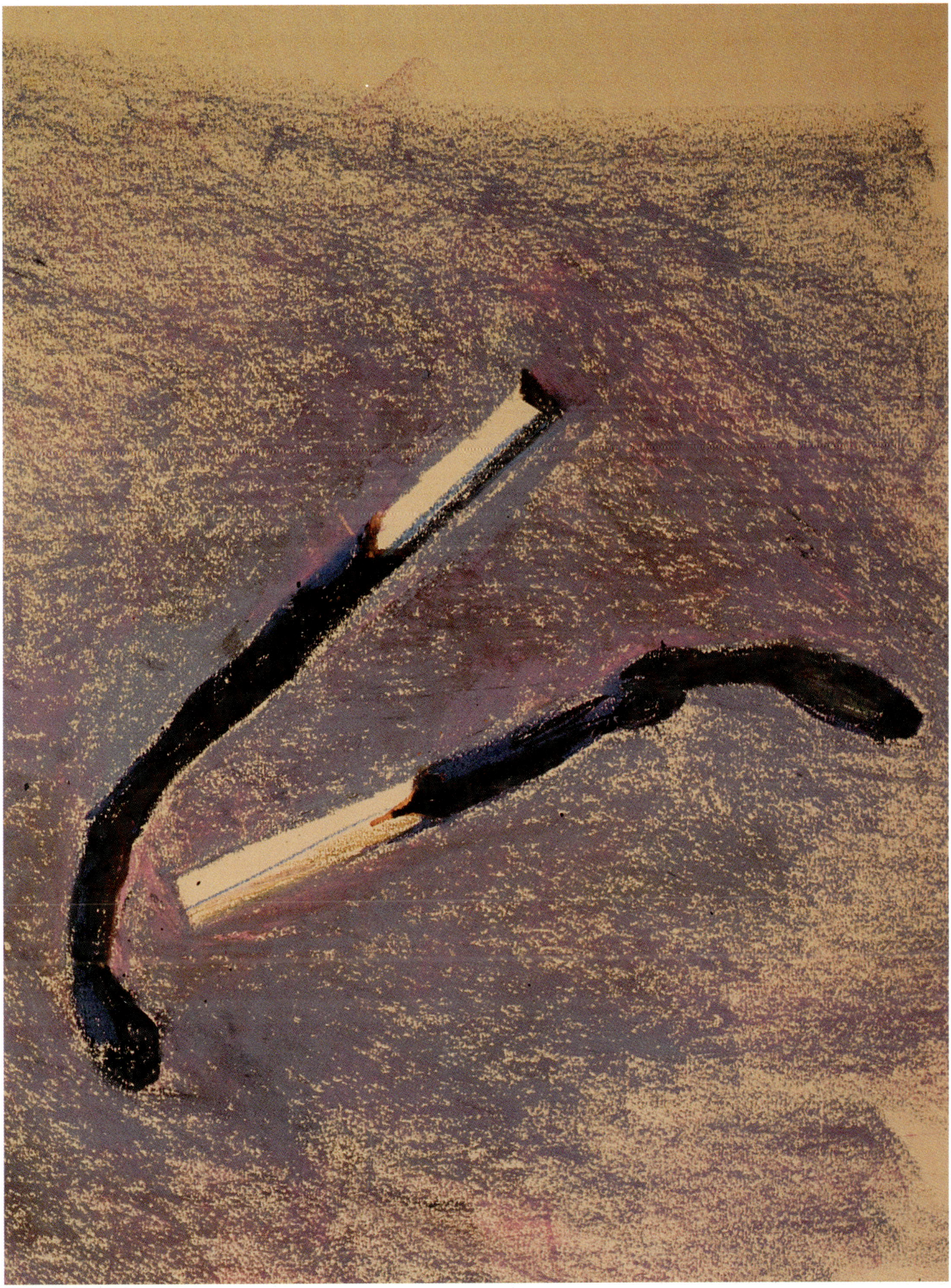

STILL LIFE WITH REFLECTIONS

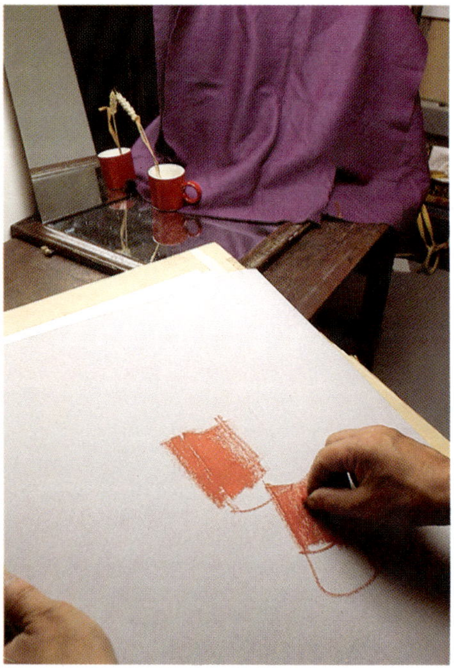

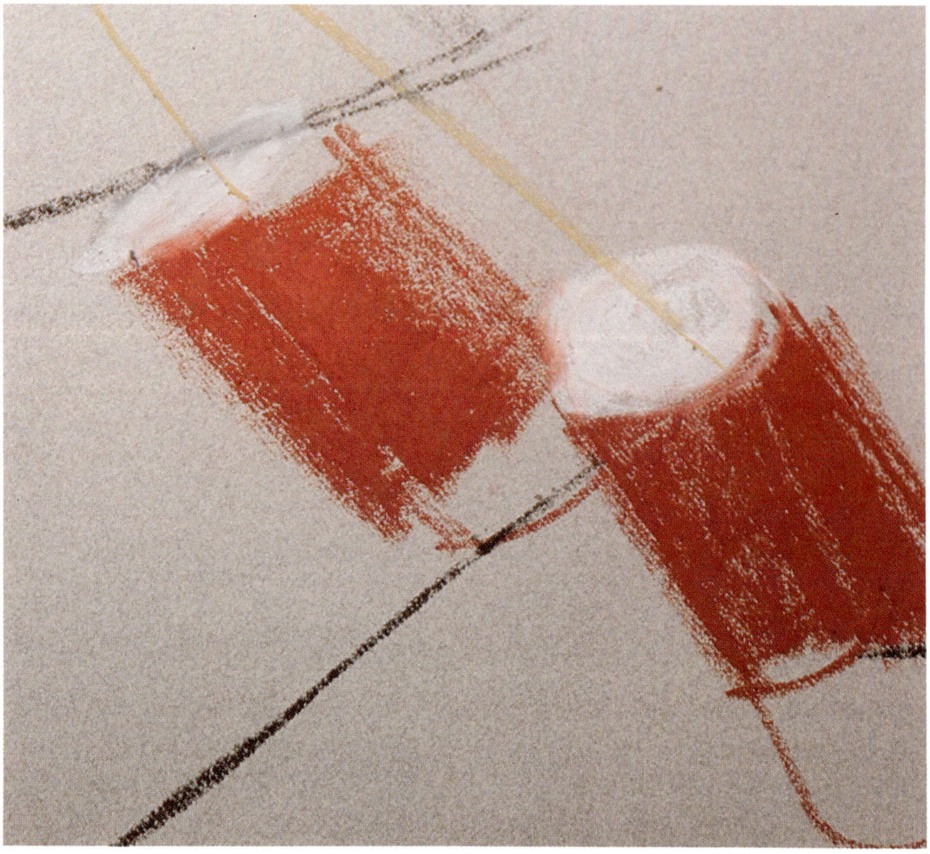

For this unusual still life the artist arranged the objects on a reflective surface. The colours of the object and the background are strong and clear. Working directly from the subject the artist concentrated on the reflections, the colours and the pattern. He selected and simplified, so that the patterns and shapes, rather than the actual representation of the objects, became the dominant theme.

He worked in pastel because it can be used at speed and he wanted to minimize the time between his eye observing the subject and his hands making a mark on the paper. He chose a grey toned paper, which had enough texture to hold the grains of pastel. Using the side of the pastel he covered the paper as broadly and flatly as possible and worked the pigment into the paper texture. Pastel has a tendency to sit on top of the paper unless it is well worked in and fixed. If you want to create a thick impasto fix each layer of pastel before applying the next layer.

The painting is composed of areas of flat colour except in the reflection where white chalk has been worked into the black to create an oily effect. The result is a fresh, brightly coloured image in which the pattern and shapes of the objects dominate — it is a very personal interpretation of the subject.

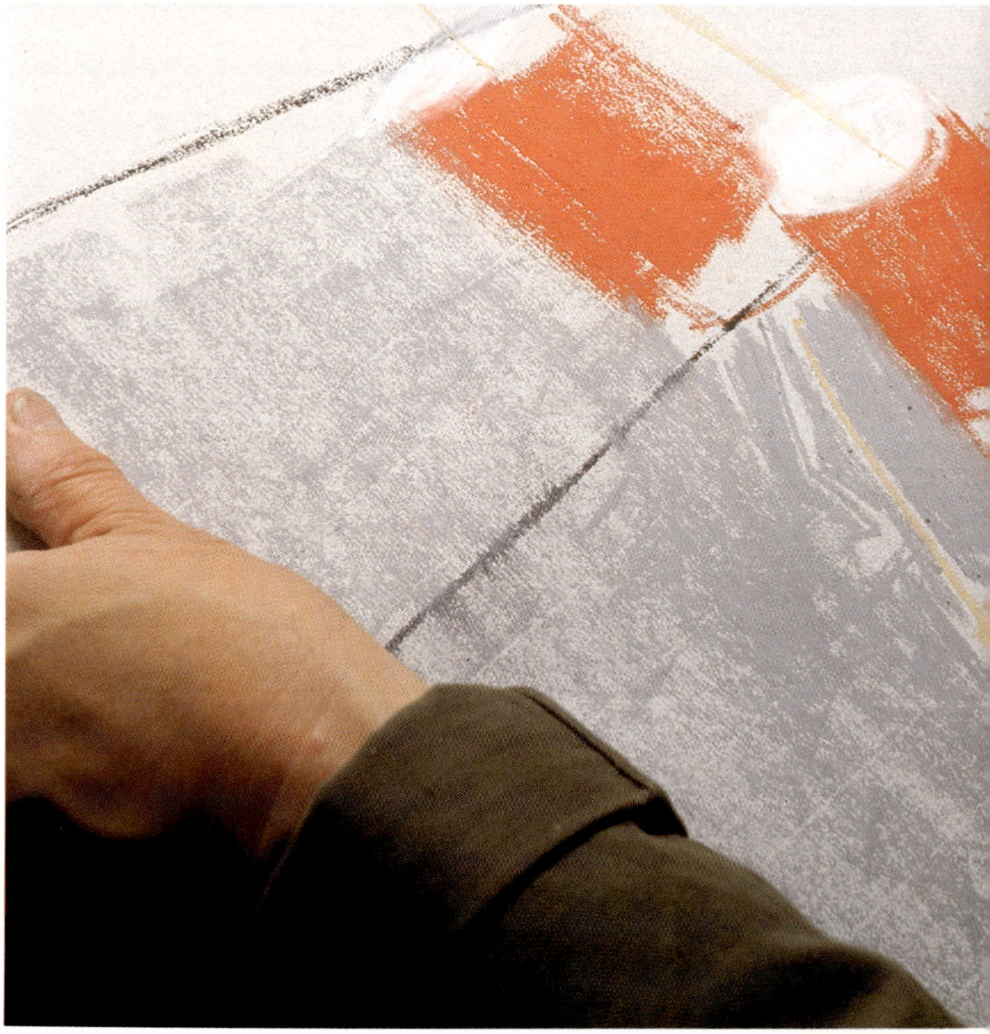

By introducing a reflective material such as glass or a mirror you can add considerable interest to your still life. The reflection introduces repeated colours and shapes, mirror images and an extra spatial dimension. The artist worked with oil pastels on tinted paper, starting with the outline of the main shapes **(far left)**. *Next he blocked in the background* **(left)** *and surrounding tones* **(below)**.

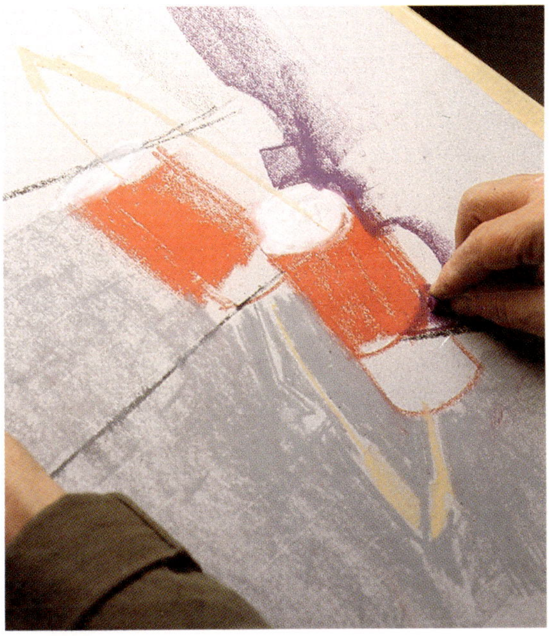

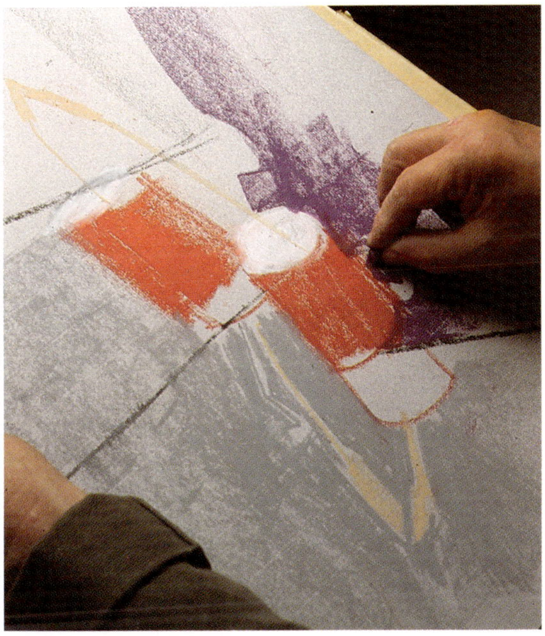

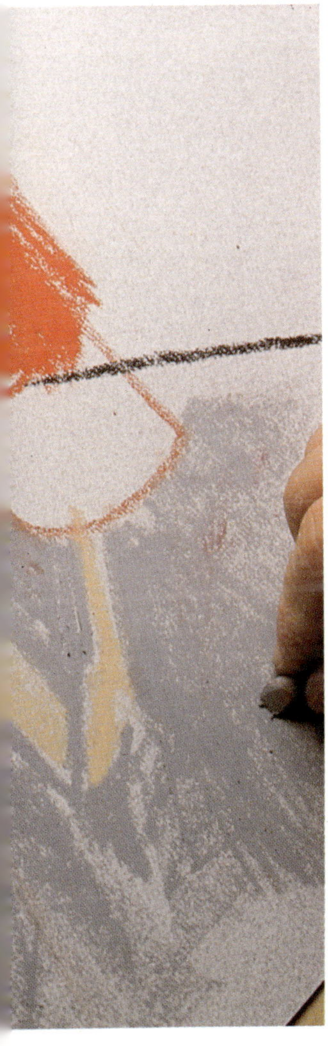

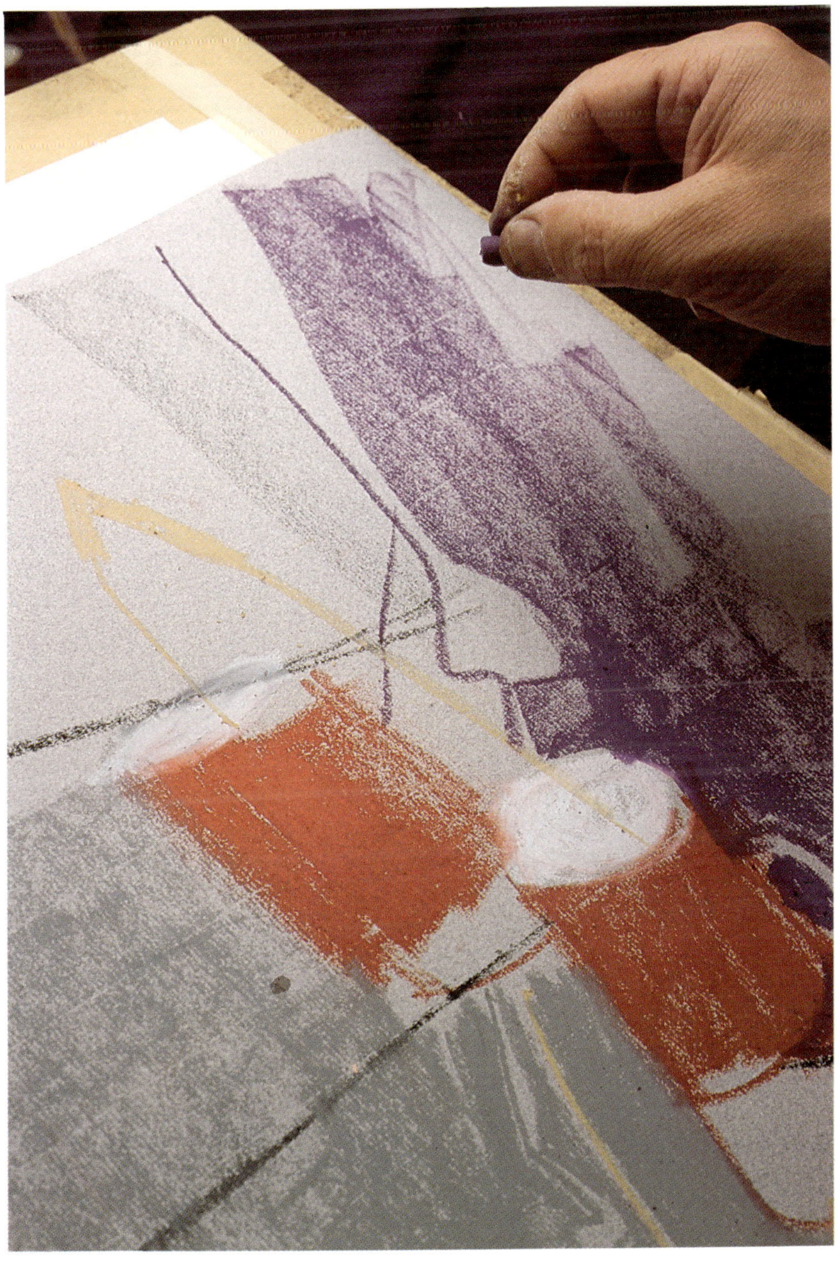

He uses the side of the pastel stick to lay in large areas of colour **(above left)**, *working into this with stronger tones to intensify the colour* **(above)**. *He takes the colour right up to the edge of the paper* **(left)**, *making the negative spaces of background into positive shapes which are important elements in the overall composition.*

1
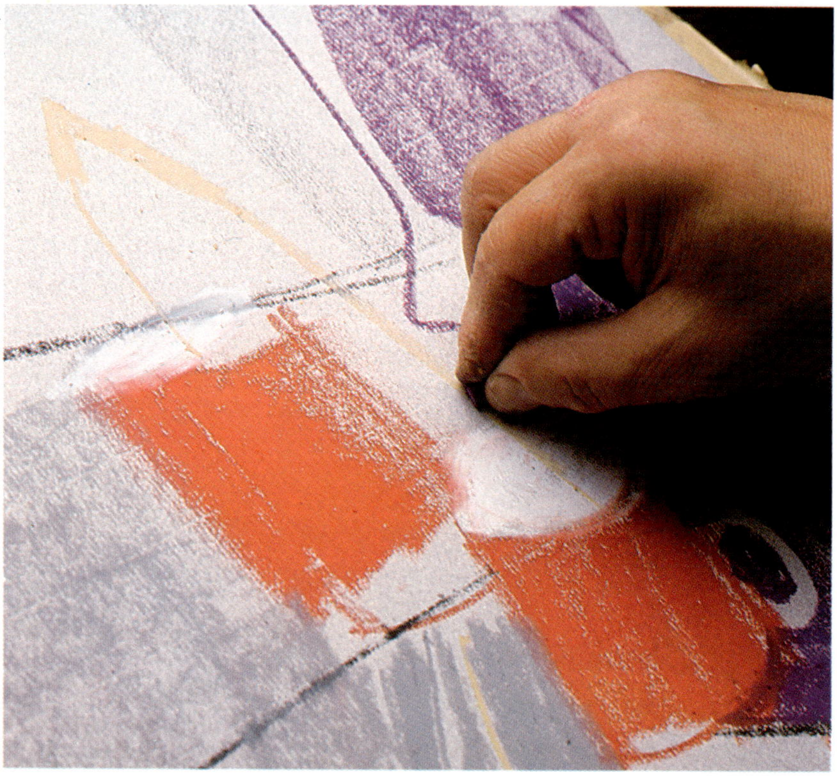

2
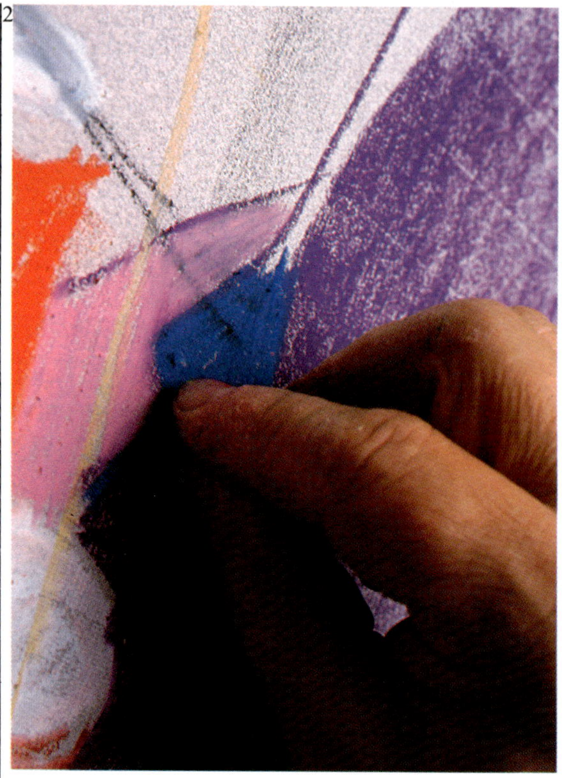

3
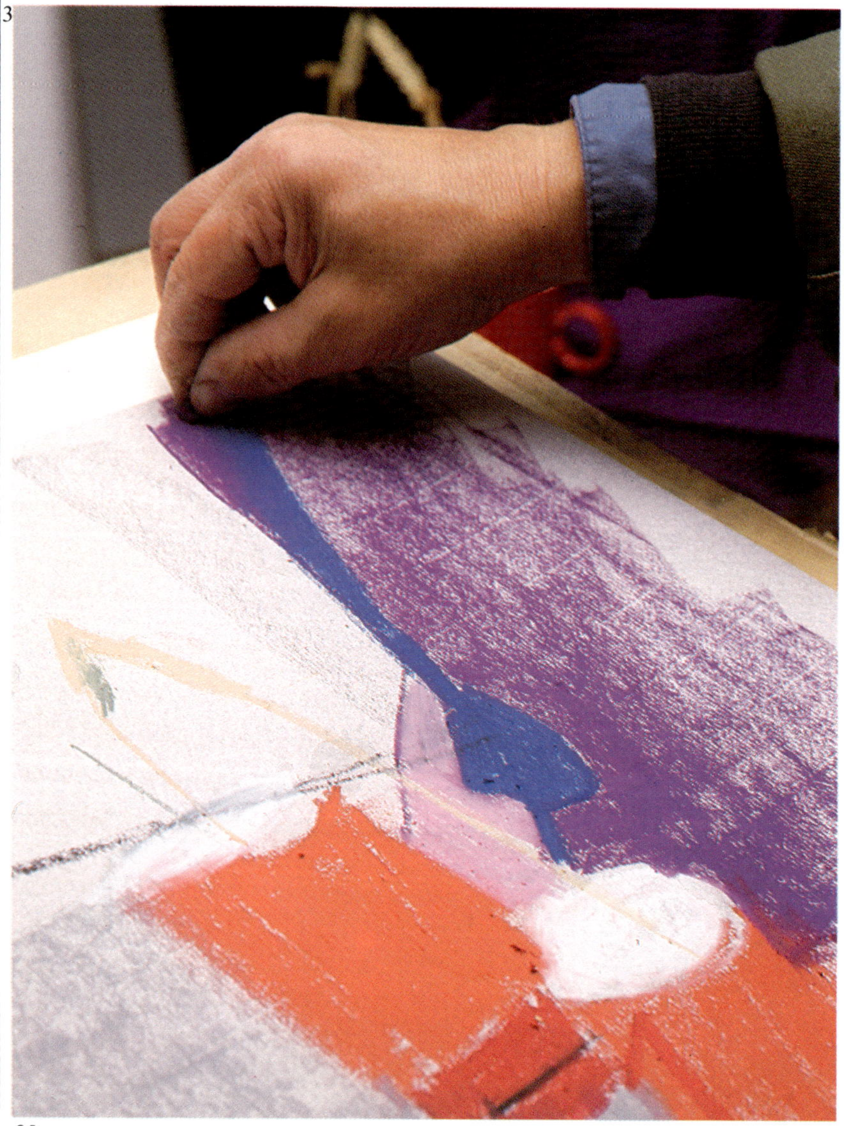

The artist continues to develop the main shapes **(above left)**, *introducing other colours to increase the vibrancy and brilliance of the composition* **(above)**. *He keeps the colours bright and clear, avoiding the mistake of overworking the drawing or clogging the paper with too many layers of pastel. Again he extends the large background shapes to the edge of the composition* **(left)**. *He defines smaller forms and details with a sharpened pastel but does not lose sight of the overall design* **(below)**. *By bringing the background colour right up to the objects he achieves a sharp, clear edge.*

4
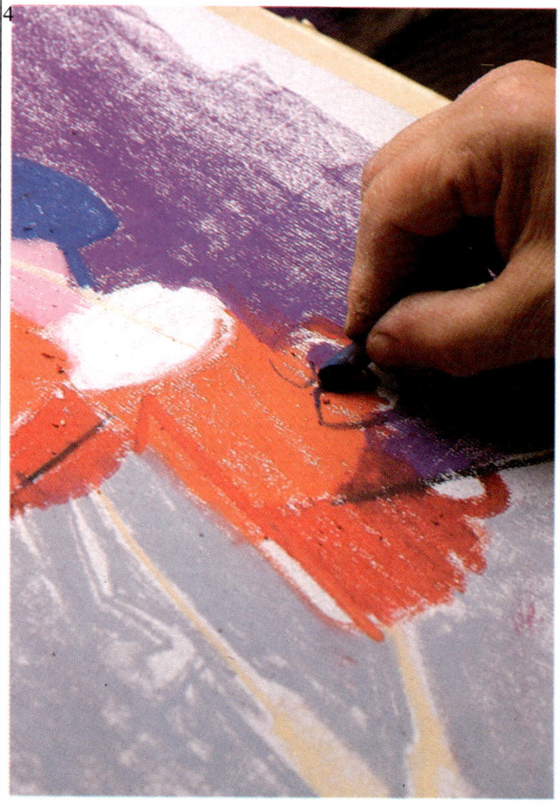

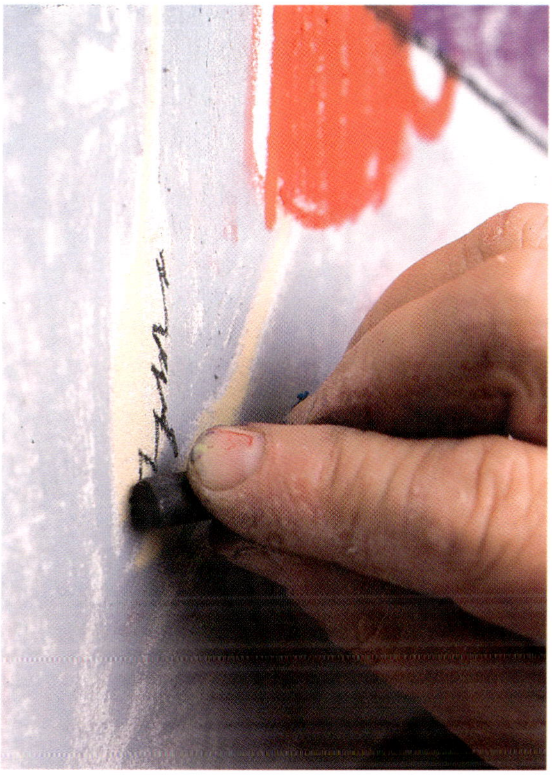

The artist uses black pastel to create darker tones and to define smaller objects and linear details **(left)**. *He then develops the highlight areas using white pastel* **(right)**. *Having increased the tonal contrasts he enriches the areas of local colour by adding black lines, treating the image and its reflection as a single subject* **(below)**.

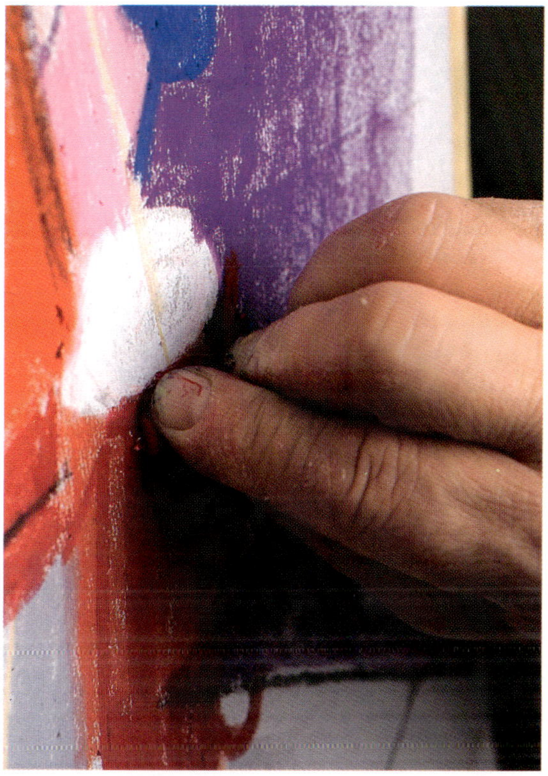

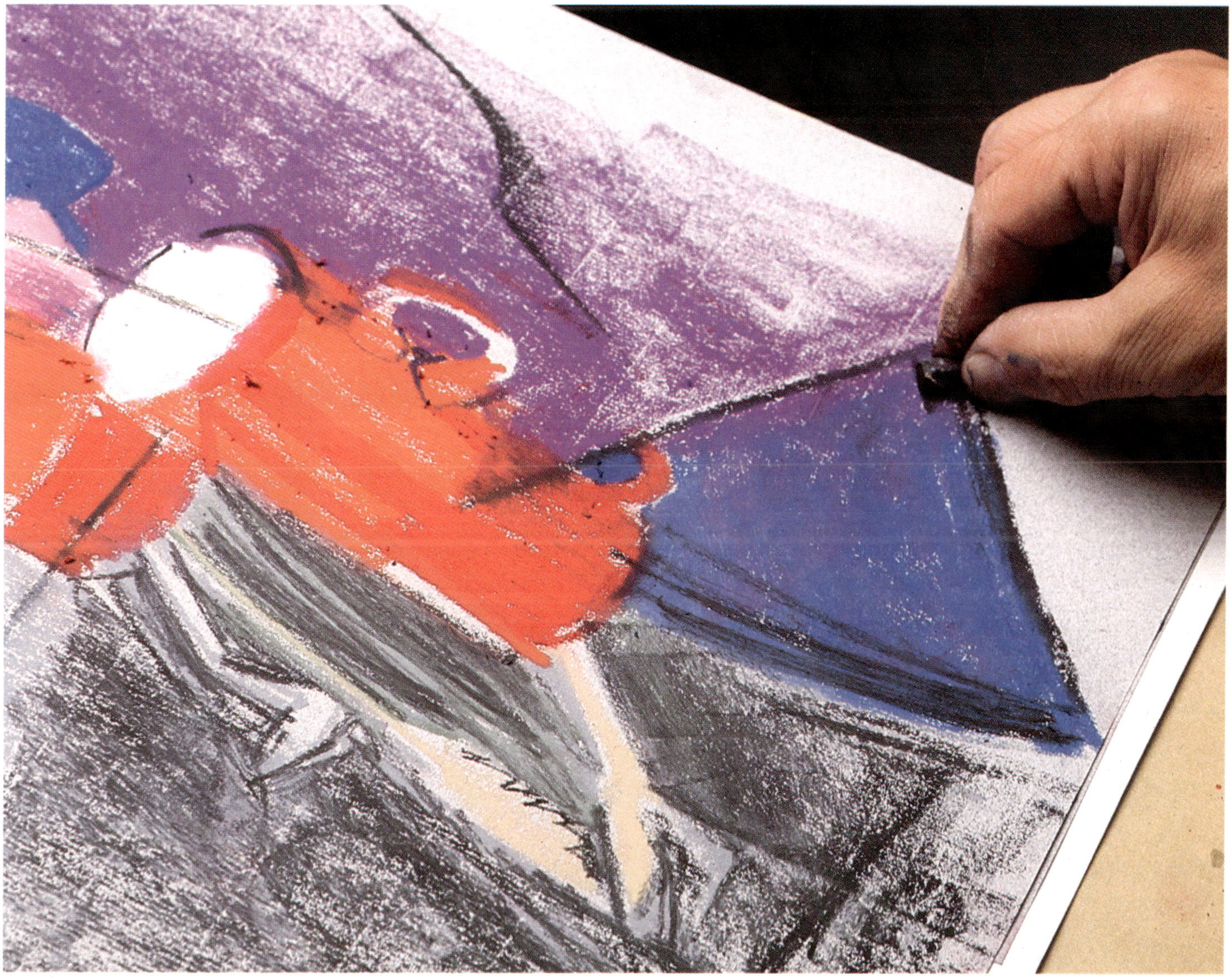

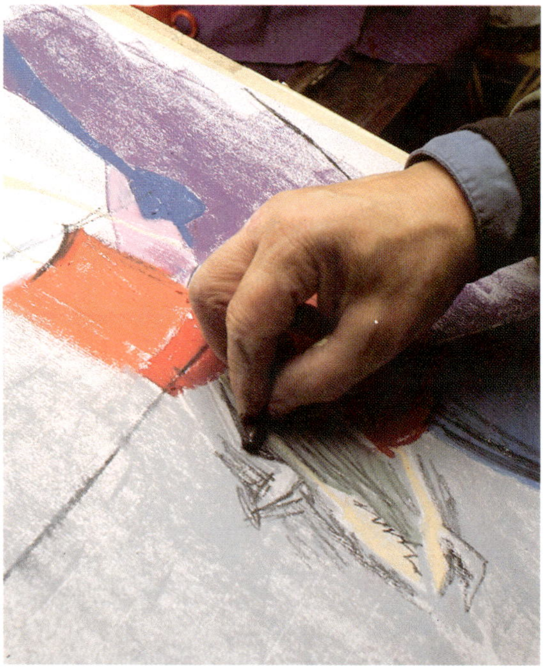

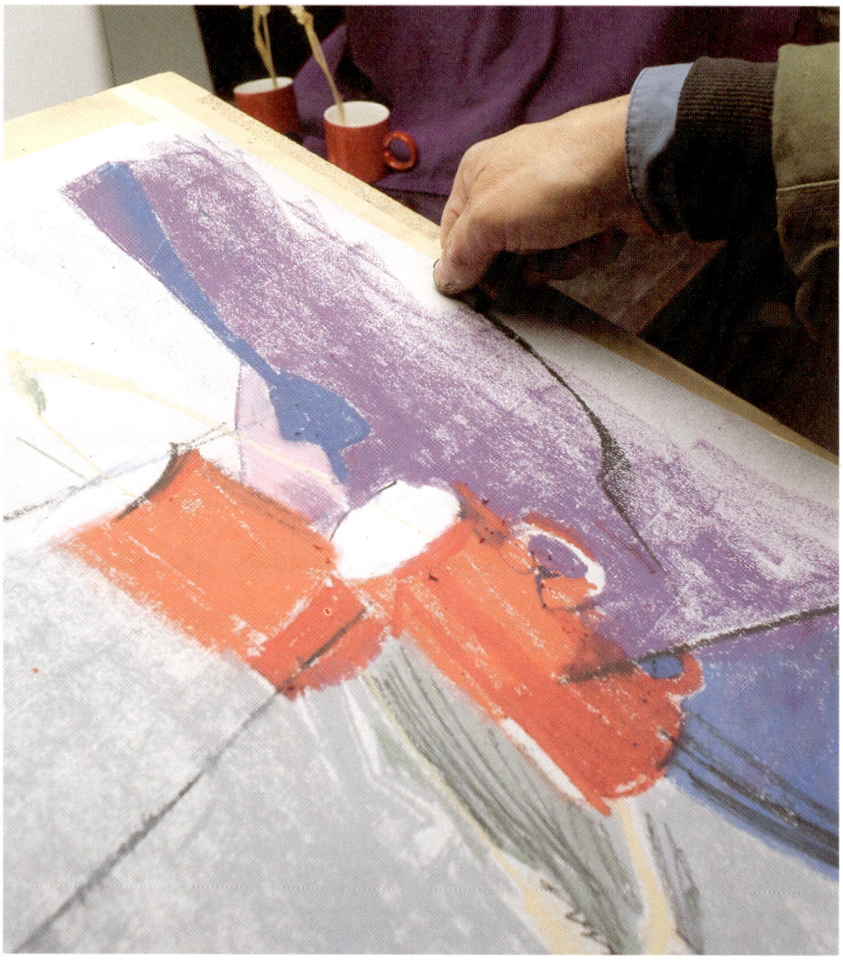

The artist continues to define the shapes and colours, constantly returning to the subject for information **(below and right)**. *The drawing is accurate but by emphasizing the areas of flat colour and the outlines he draws attention to the pattern-making qualities of the composition. He pays equal attention to the reflected images* **(above)** *making them as clear and precise as the objects themselves and creating a three-dimensional but ambiguous space.*

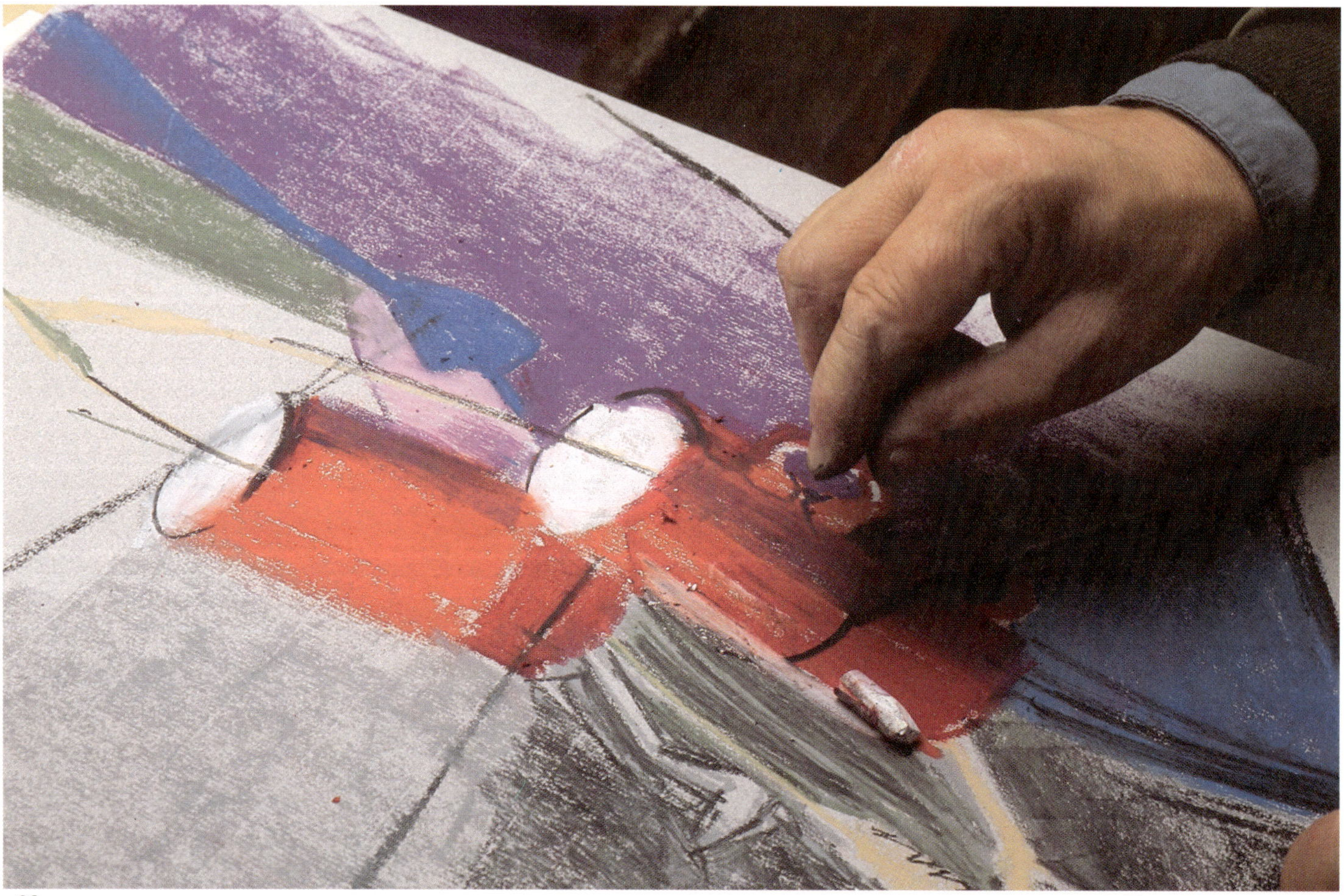

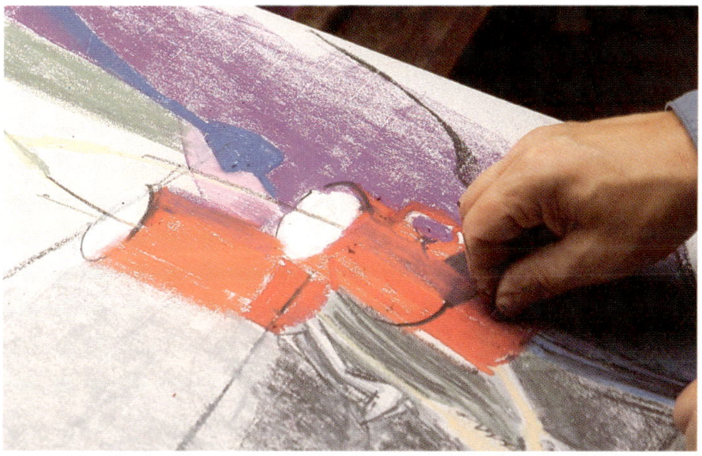

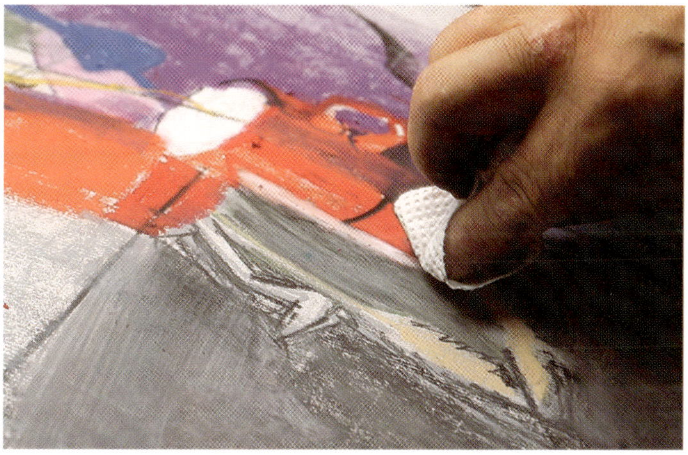

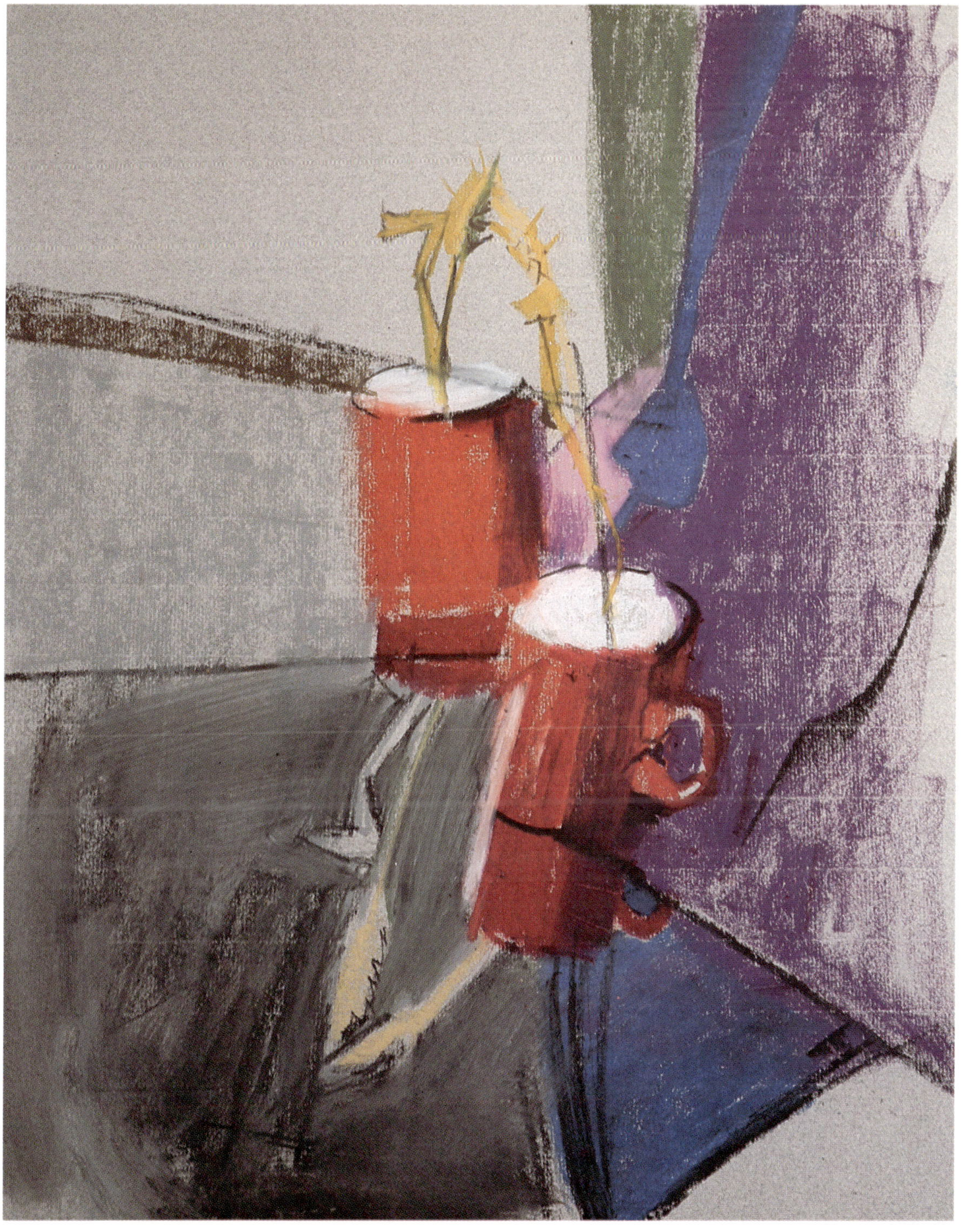

By making the reflected images deeper and richer than the actual objects, the artist implies the surface of the reflective material **(top left)**. *He buffs the picture surface with a piece of tissue, smearing the pastels to create the impression of a shiny, reflective effect* **(top right)**. *He completes the picture by drawing a fine black line of shadow between the objects and their mirror image* **(bottom)**.

TWO PORTRAITS

Pastels are an especially sensitive medium to use for figure and portrait work — with their velvety bloom and softness they suit the delicate textures and tones of flesh. Selecting a suitable range of colours is very much a matter of personal taste. All the major manufacturers sell sets of colours designed specifically for figure work and faced with the daunting task of selecting from the great range of colours and tones you may find this the easy way out of a dilemma.

Pastels have an intimacy and immediacy of presentation which makes many people think that they are somehow dashed off in a very short time. This, as you will soon discover, is an illusion. A letter from the artist la Tour (1704–1788) to the Marquis de Marigny, the brother of Mme de Pompadour, is reassuring, for it lists the same difficulties as anyone working with the medium today will experience.

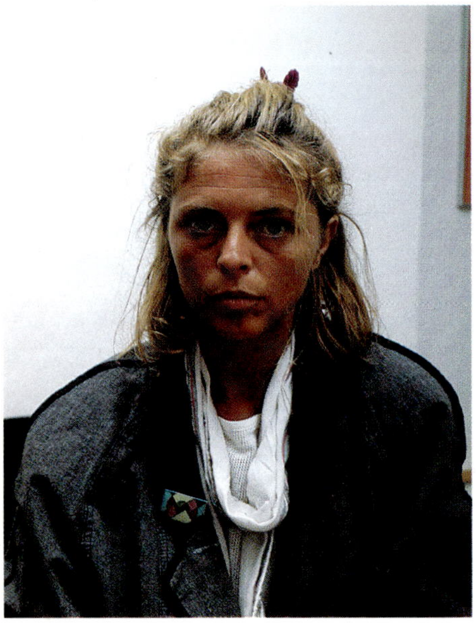

'Pastels, my Lord Marquis, involve a number of further obstacles, such as dust, the weakness of some pigments, the fact that the tone is never correct, that one must blend one's colours on the paper and apply a number of strokes with different crayons instead of one, that there is a risk of spoiling the work done and that one has no expedient if the spirit is lost...'

The problem of having to apply a number of strokes with different crayons instead of one is very real. For this reason it is important to lay the pastels out in a methodical order on corrugated paper rather than in the box, and to replace them in their correct positions. There is nothing more irritating if you are in full spate than to have to stop work to search for the missing colour.

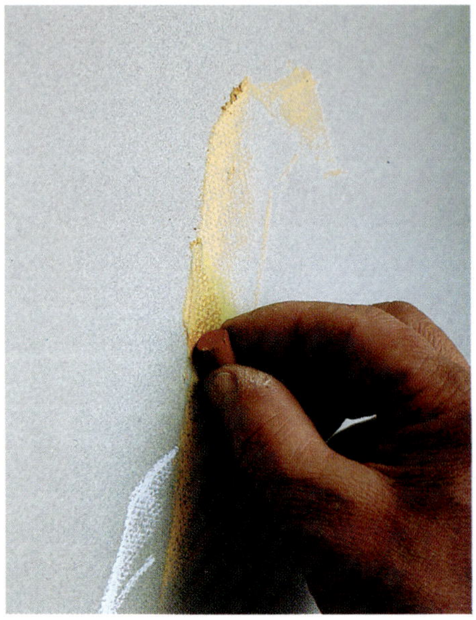

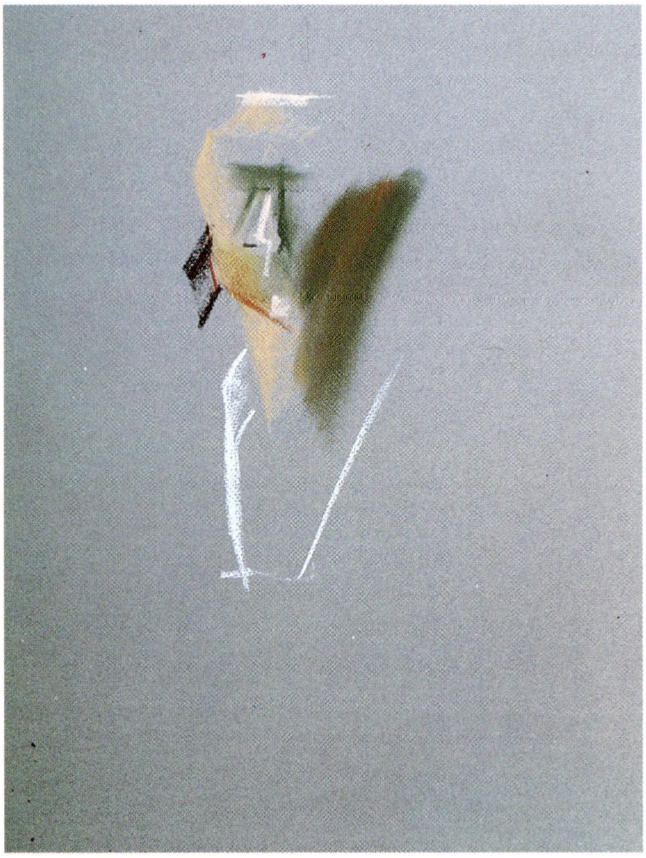

The artist wanted to make a rapid drawing of the model **(far left)** *to be used as the basis of a portrait at a later date. He chose to work with pastel because it is soft and responsive, lines and solid colours building up rapidly to create an effective image. It also provides him with plenty of colour reference.*

He chose a tinted paper because this gives him a useful mid-tone and the opaque pigments show to advantage on a coloured ground. Selecting a flesh tinted pastel he starts to block in the lighter tones of the face **(top left** *and* **right)**.

With white he indicates the position of the main features and the broad outlines of the girl's clothing. At the same time he develops the darkest areas by smudging in greeny-brown pigment **(left)**.

With his finger he uses the same pigment to lay in the shadowy areas of the eye sockets and the side of the nose **(right)**.

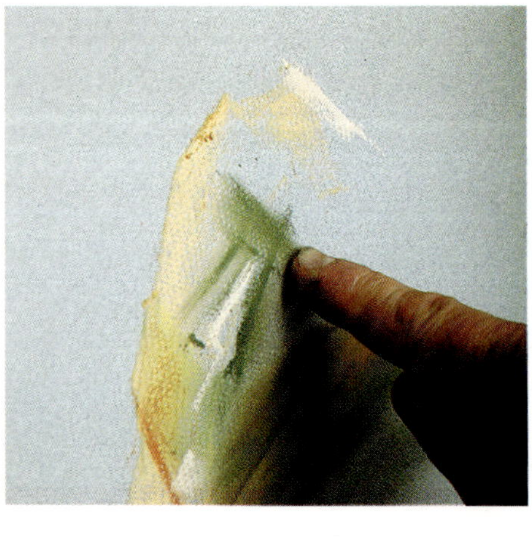

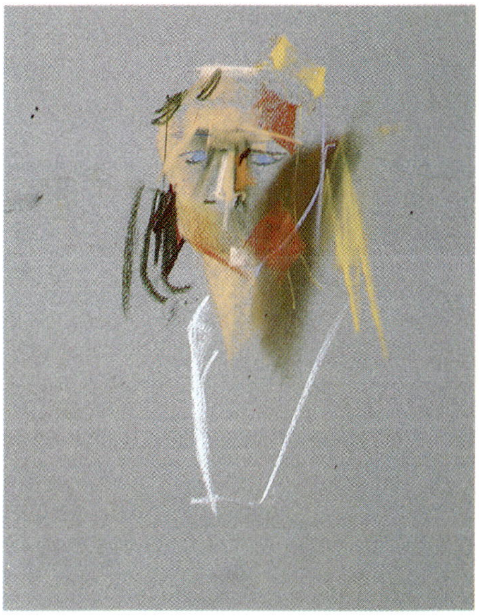

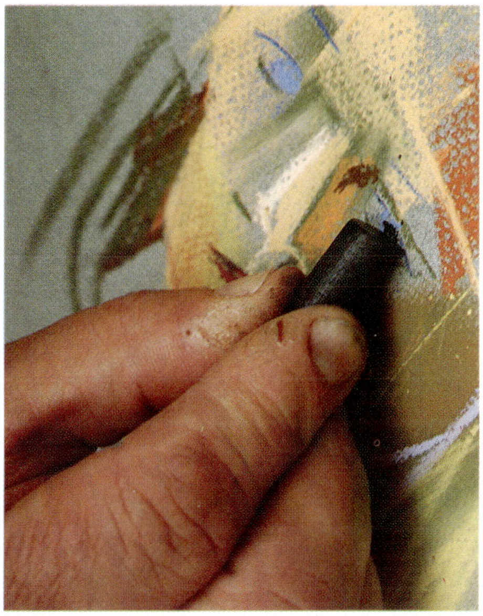

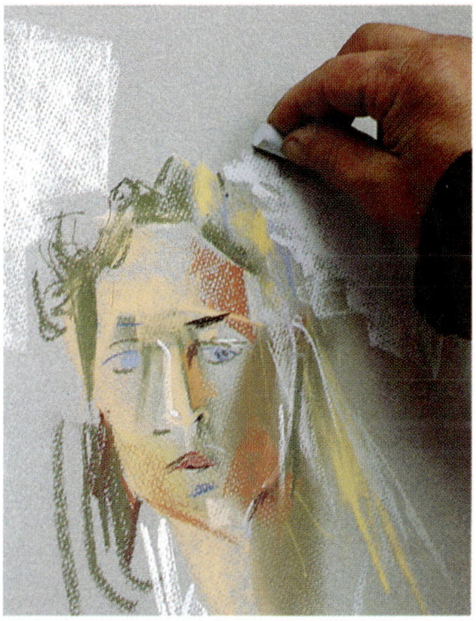

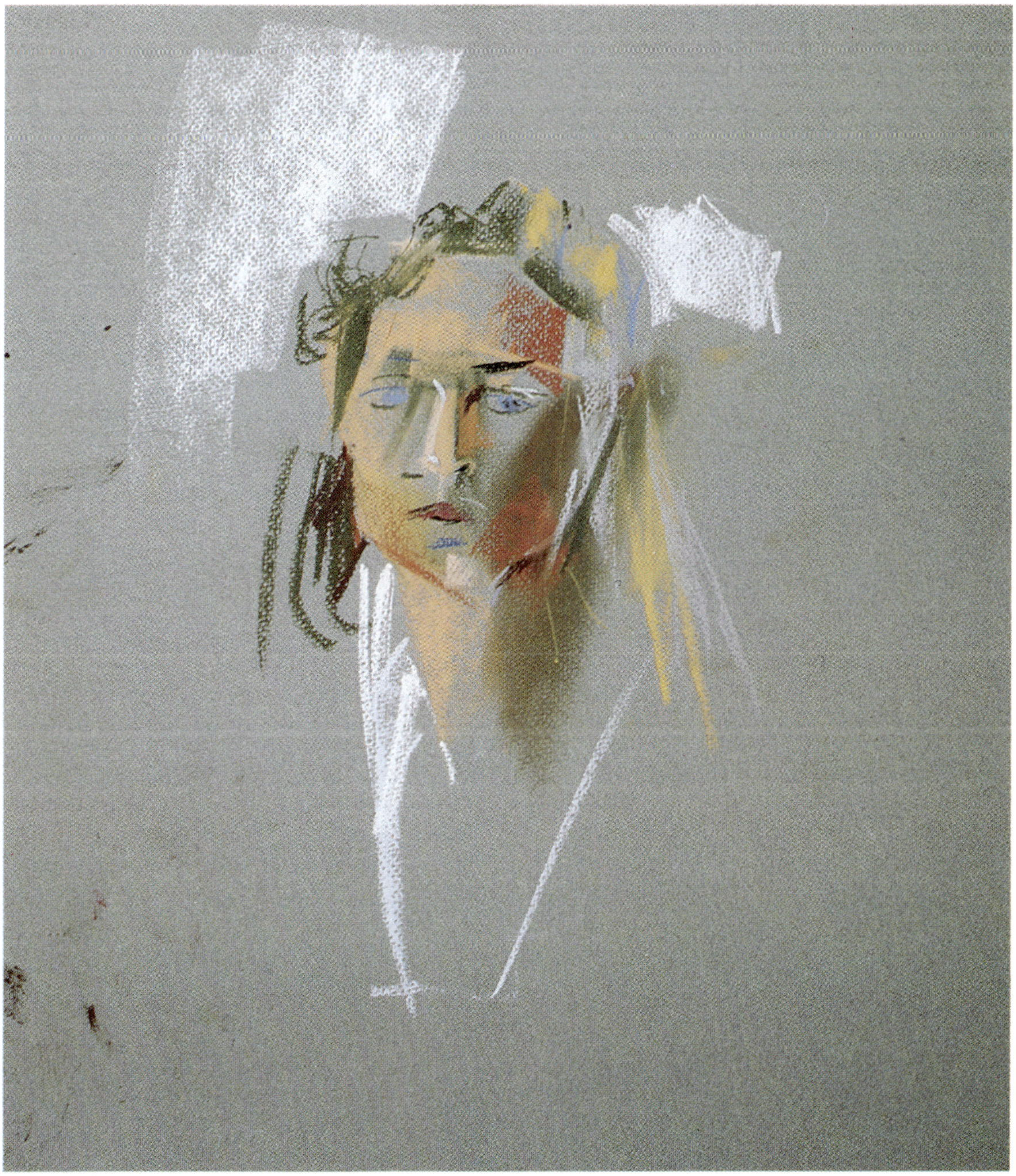

The artist continues to work broadly and quickly, adding broad strokes of warm tones to the head and hair, half-closing his eyes to help him isolate the lights and darks **(top left)**. *With a black pastel he defines some of the features — the eyes, nose and eyebrows* **(above centre)**. *He uses the side of the pastel to lay in broad planes of colour, brick red and flesh tint describing the facets of the forehead. With a white pastel he starts to scumble in the background, the tinted ground modifying the white pigment* **(left)**. *He continues to develop the background using the side of a grey pastel to create patches of solid colour* **(above)**. *He uses a black pastel to strengthen the darker tones, drawing with the sharpened tip of the stick and laying in broader areas of colour with the side of the stick. Finally he blends the background whites and greys by rubbing them lightly with his finger* **(over)**.

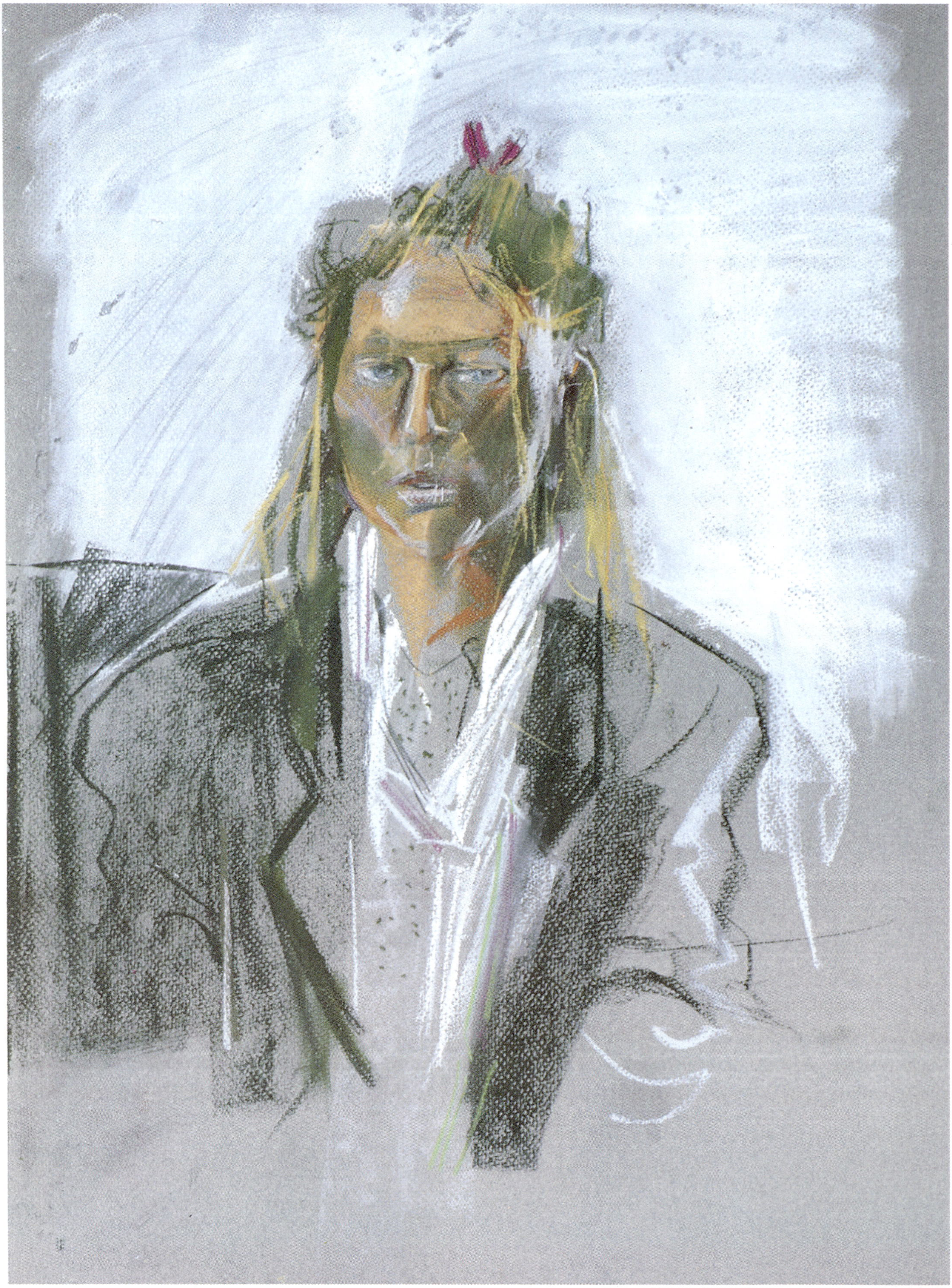

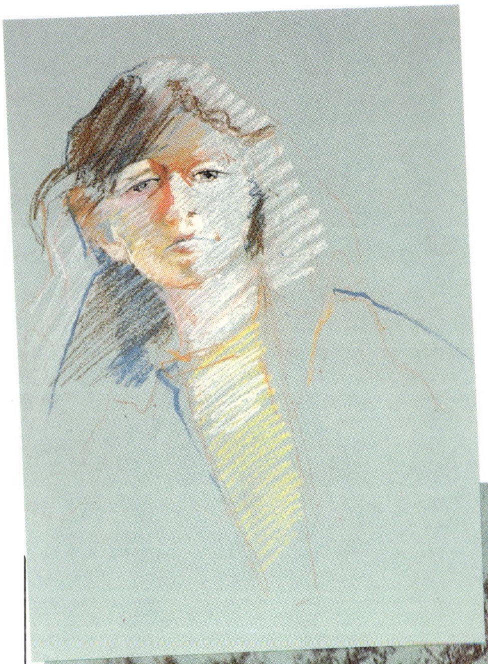

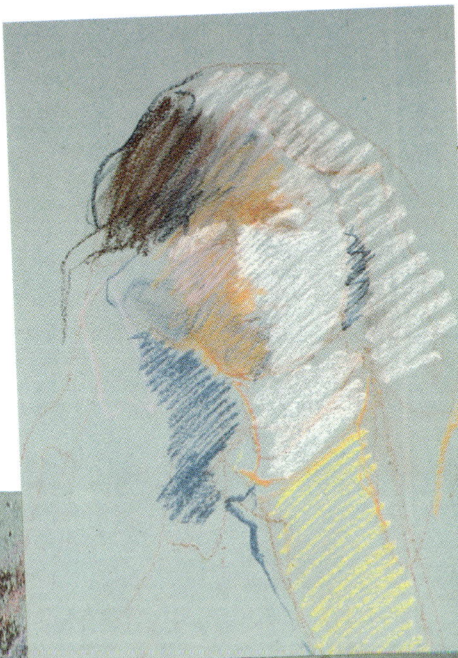

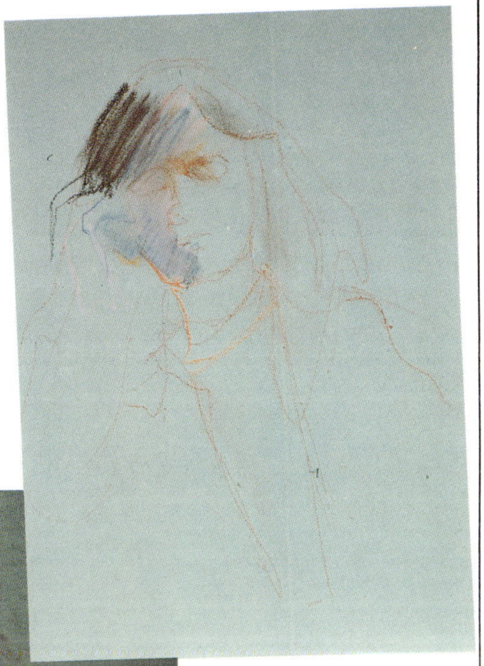

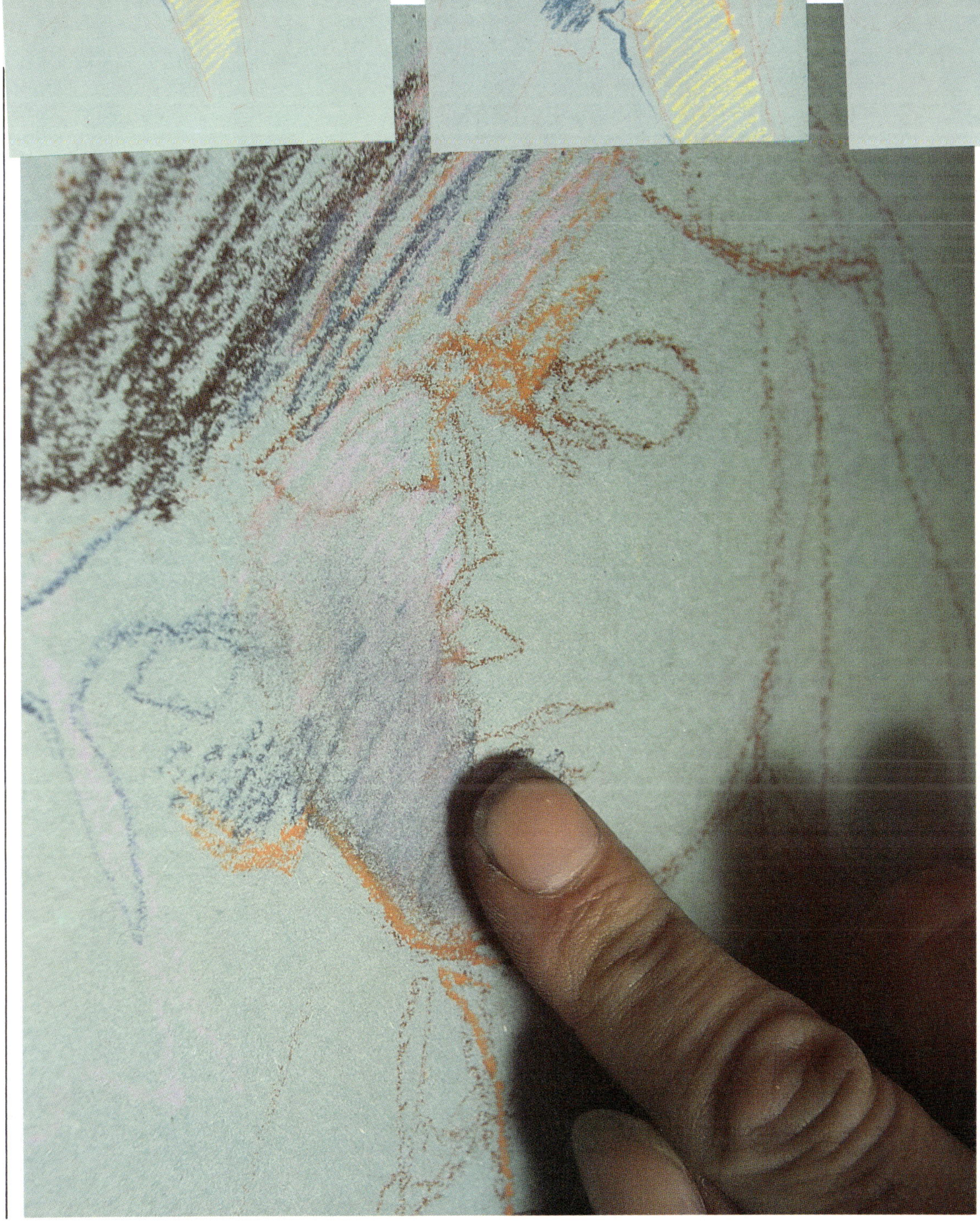

Again the artist wanted to capture the character of the subject in a quick sketch. The artist used a vigorous, calligraphic style, the direction of the rapidly hatched strokes helping to establish the bulk of the forms. He starts by drawing the broad outlines of the figure in burnt sienna. He then works into the face with loosely hatched areas of bright orange, ultramarine and pink, with dark brown used for the hair **(left)**. *With his finger he lightly blends these tones to provide a sort of underpainting* **(above)**.

With white pastel he hatches in the light tones where the light catches the side of the face. With a warm yellow he scribbles in the front of the torso, while a cool blue is used for the background and the shadows between skull and hair **(top left)**.

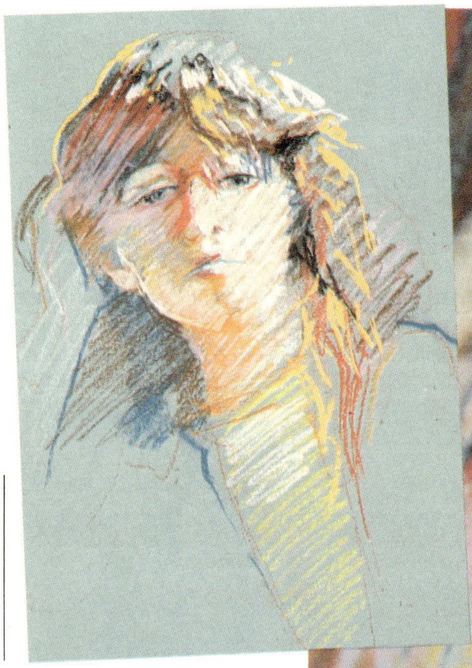

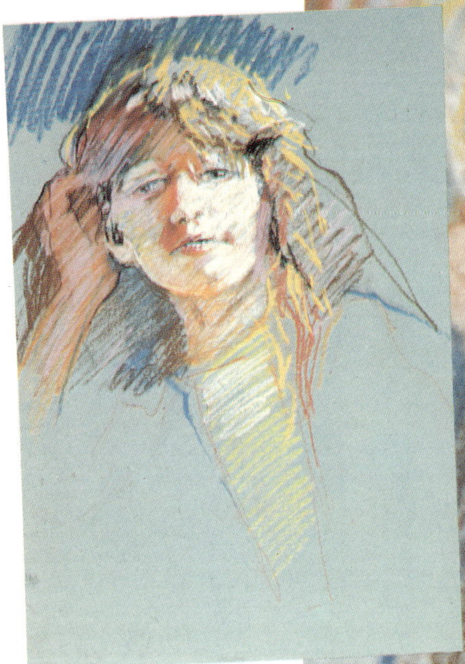

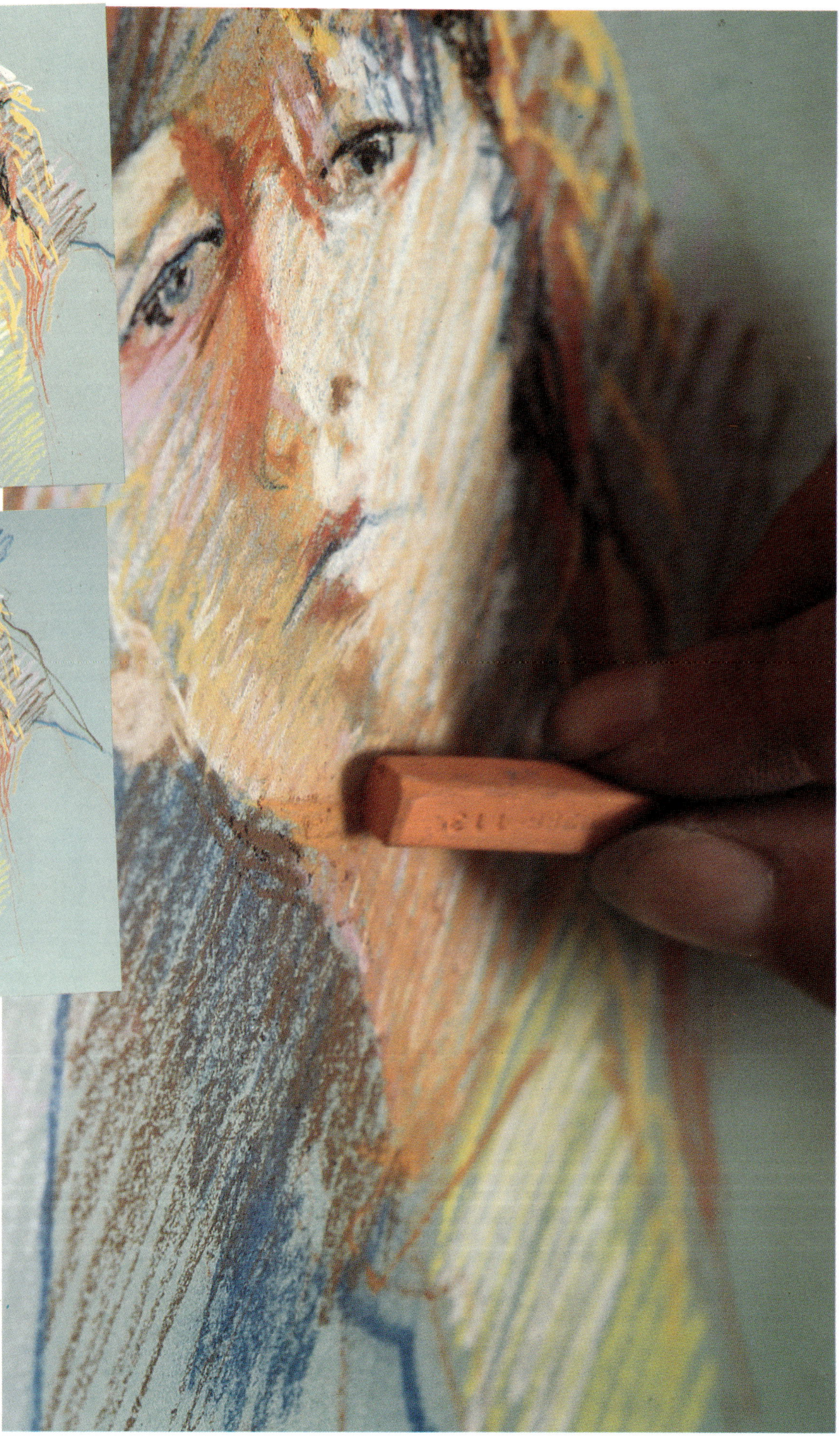

The artist sees the figure in terms of lights and darks, warm colours and cool colours. He uses a creamy colour for the bright side of the face laying it over the blended white. With black he draws back into the figure to re-establish the outlines of the head and hair **(top)**. *Black is also used to draw the right hand and arm, and the dark flesh tones are orange and mauve* **(above)**.

Warm and cool colours are superimposed to create a vibrant, exciting image which is established through the activity of the colour rather than the meticulous delineation of forms **(right** *and* **opposite)**.

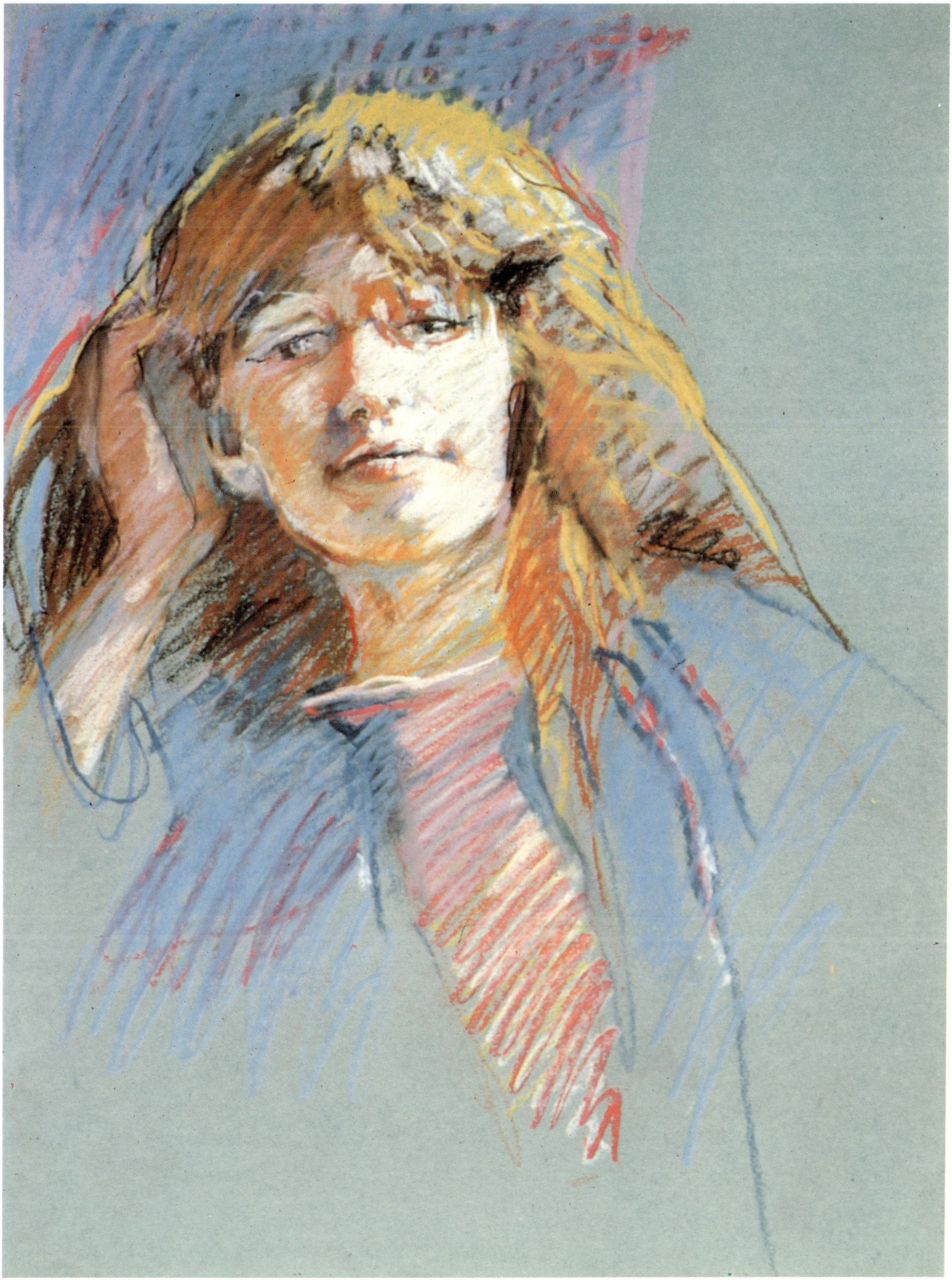

DEVELOPING A COMPOSITION

If you have not used pastel before, you can start with a very small range of colours, four will be quite sufficient; black, white, red and brown. Rectangular black, sanguine and brown Conté crayons are very useful for preliminary drawings and for accenting lines. If you select a larger range choose a light, medium and dark tone of each colour. Note, also, that the tint charts accompanying the boxed sets are printed on white paper, so that for work on darker or coloured paper it is best to make your own tint chart.

The artist made this sketch on tinted paper using a very small range of colours. He was developing material for a large figurative painting. He laid down colour in broad smudgy areas, investigating the main shapes and the way the elements occupied the picture area and related to each other. The colour areas were discrete, softly blended at the margins, rather than overlaid to create new colours. Used in this way the purity of the pigment is shown to great advantage, the freshness of the colour having much in common with pure watercolour. The sketch started as an investigation but the finished drawing is a delightful and satisfying piece in its own right.

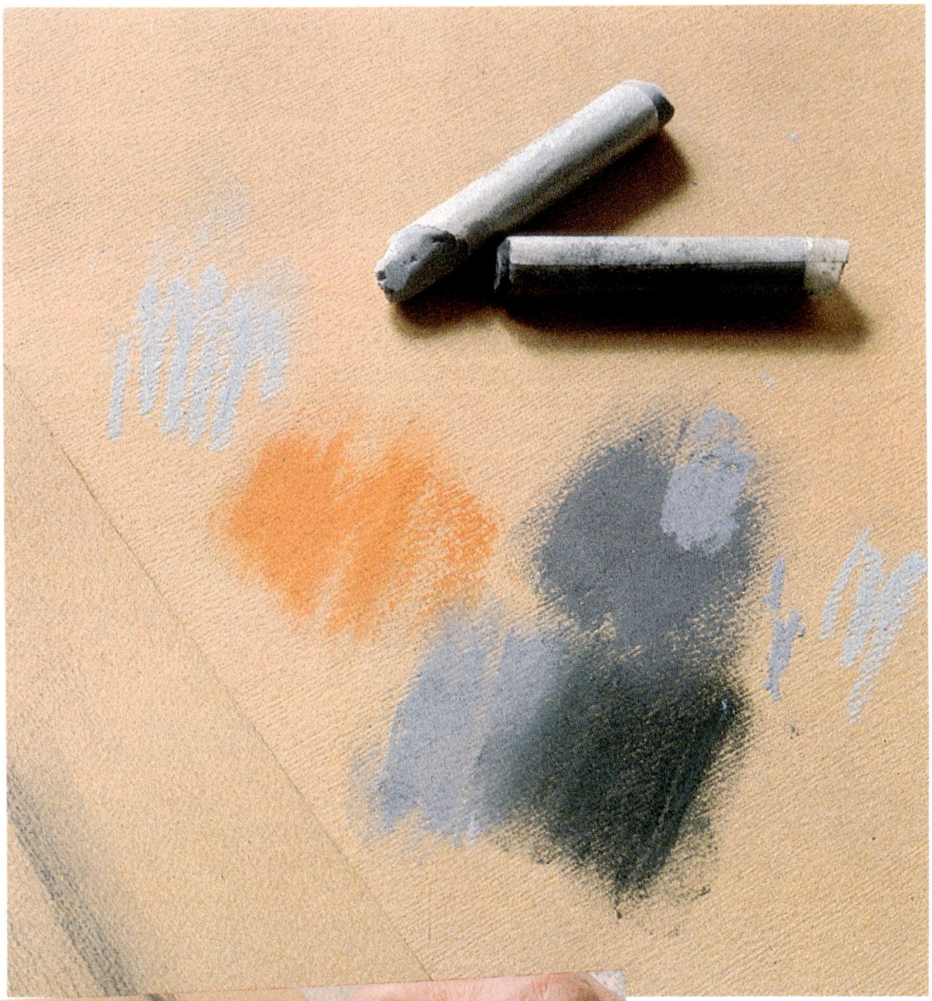

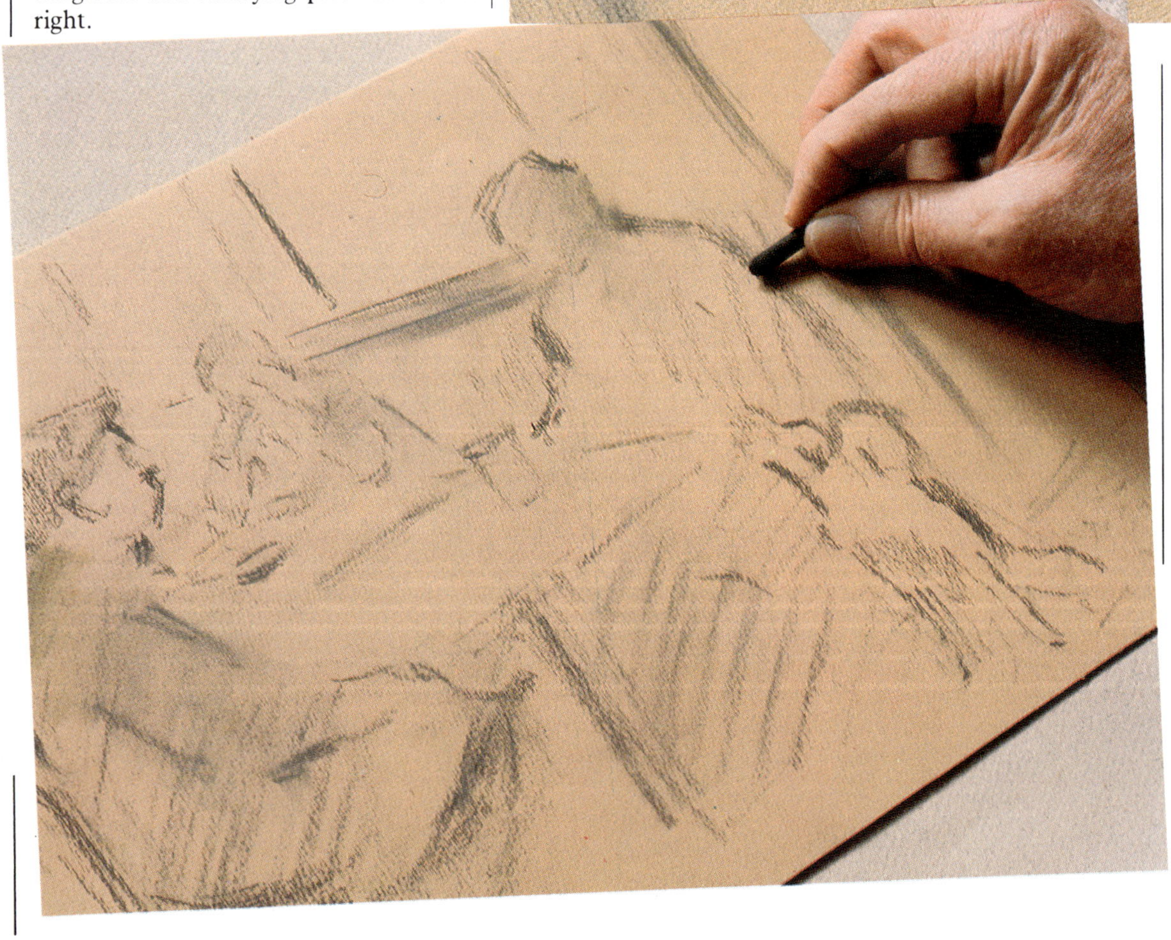

The artist starts by roughing out the broad outlines of the image with a piece of thin willow charcoal **(left)**. *Charcoal is a pleasant drawing medium with a responsive fluid line. It combines well with pastel and Degas often combined the two mediums in his pastel drawings and paintings.*

He tries his colours on a piece of paper of the same colour as his support, this enables him to select a range of suitable colours **(top)**. *It is not always possible to recognize a pastel colour in the stick — the darker tones especially are very difficult to identify.*

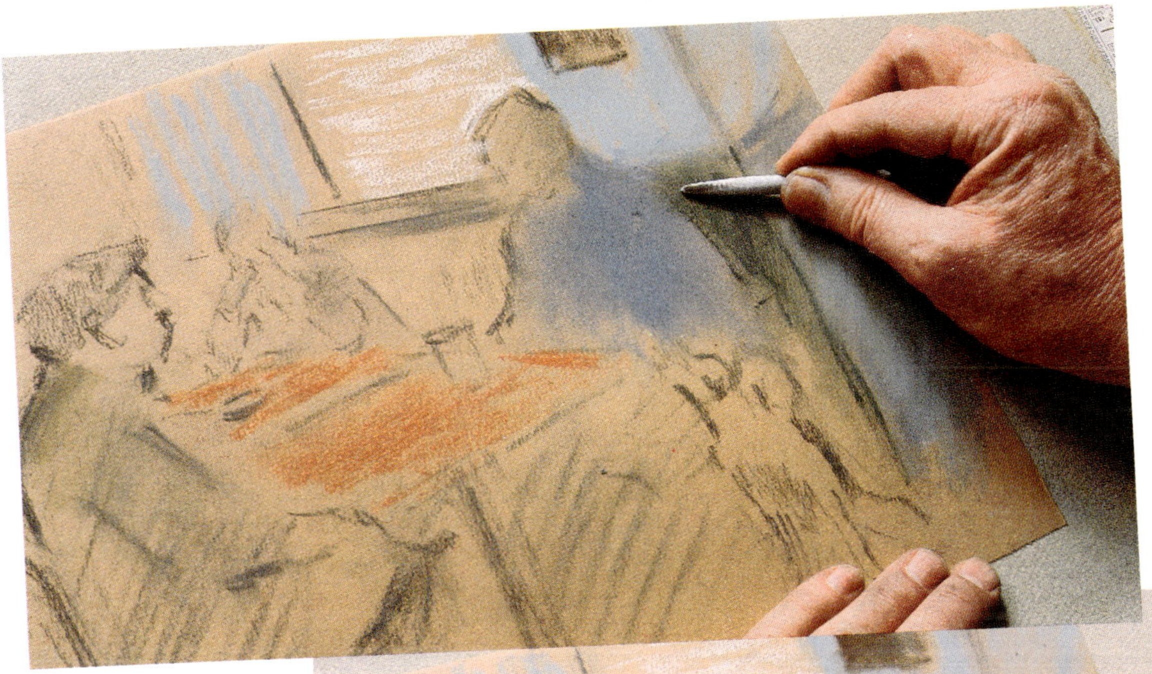

The artist starts to lay in the main areas, at this stage he keeps the pigment layer very thin. He uses a light grey coloured pencil to develop the broad form of the dog which is simply rendered using loosely hatched lines **(left)**.

He starts to lay down the colours, concentrating on the lights and darks, the contrasts, the edges between areas and the background spaces. Gradually the image emerges from the massed colours and tonal areas. The torchon is used to spread the colours thinly **(below)**.

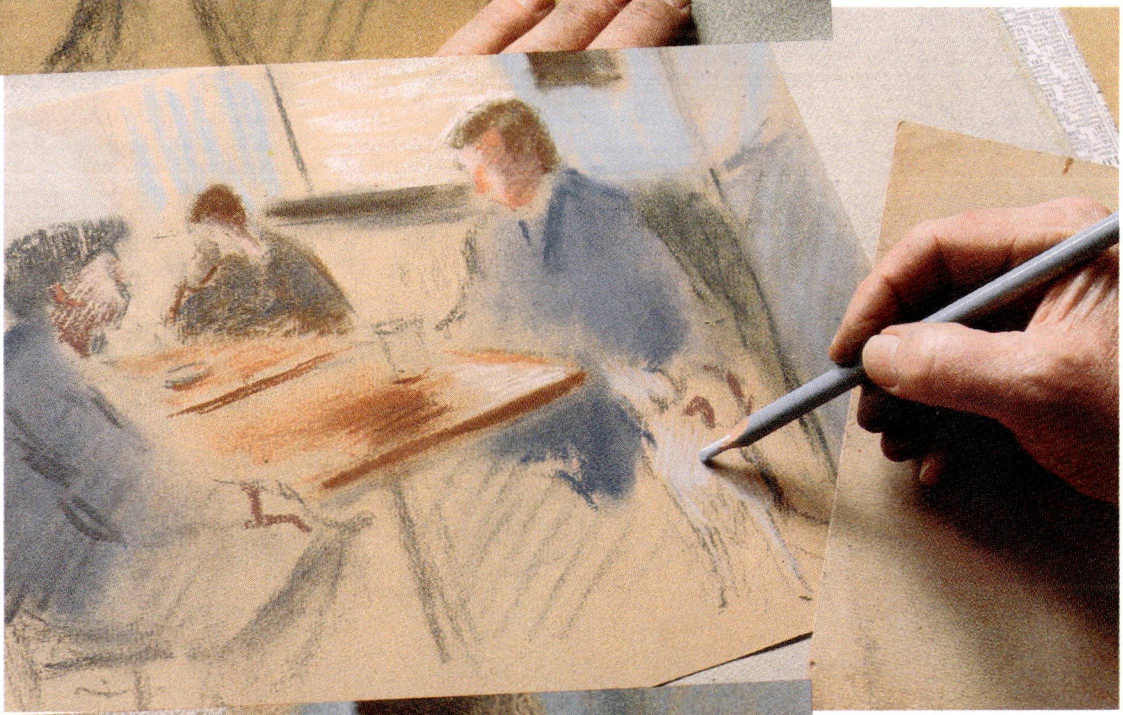

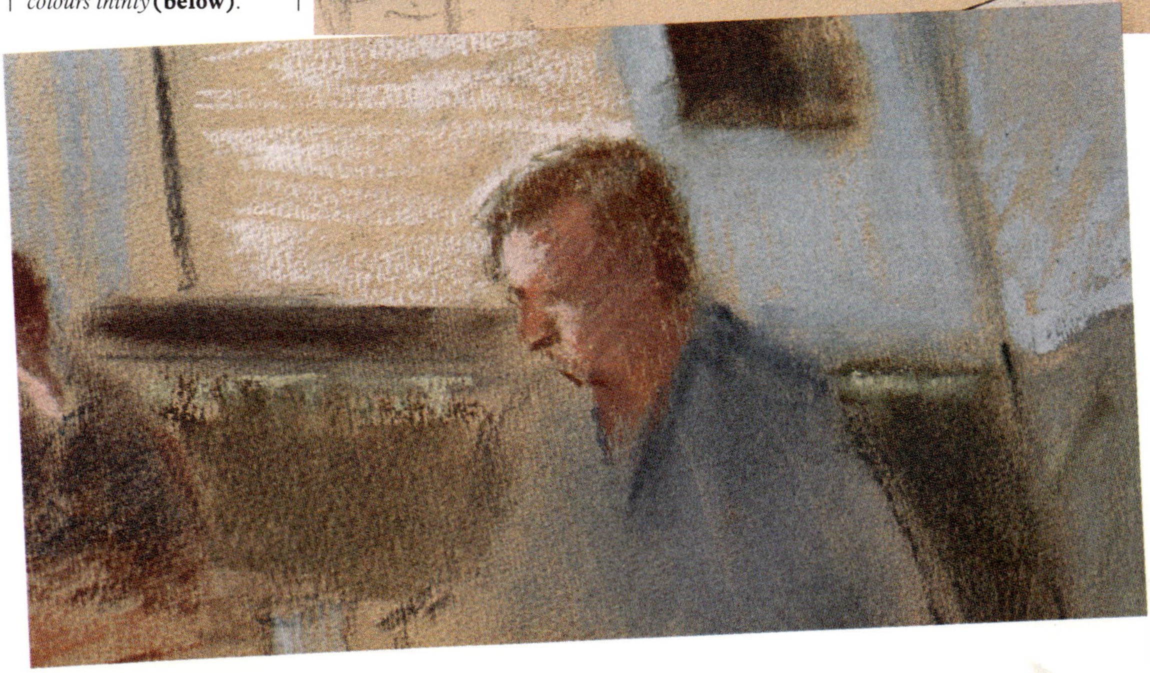

He continues to work into the drawing, identifying the darkest and lightest areas, and using a combination of warm and cool colours to give the image a lively, atmospheric feeling **(above)**.

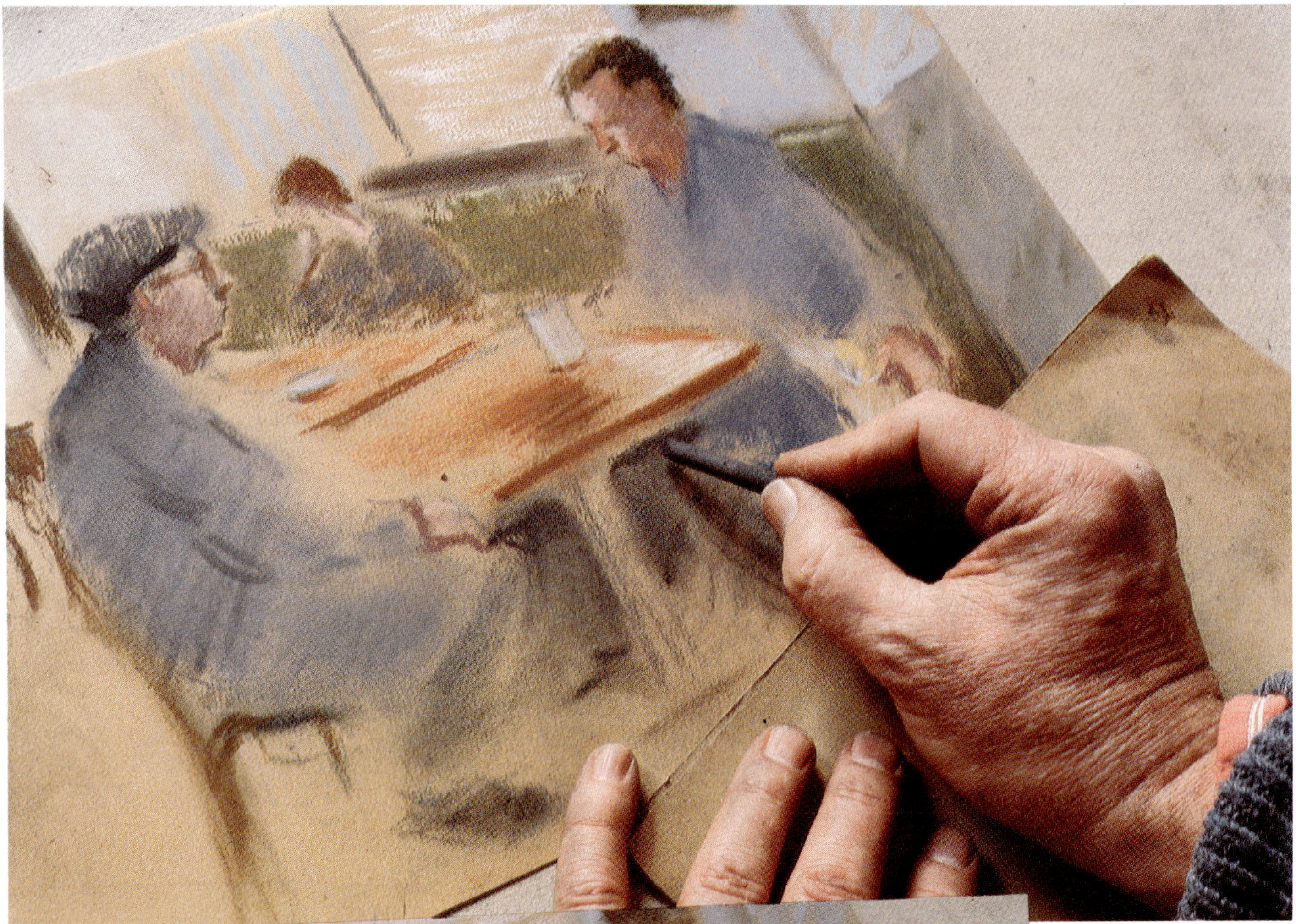

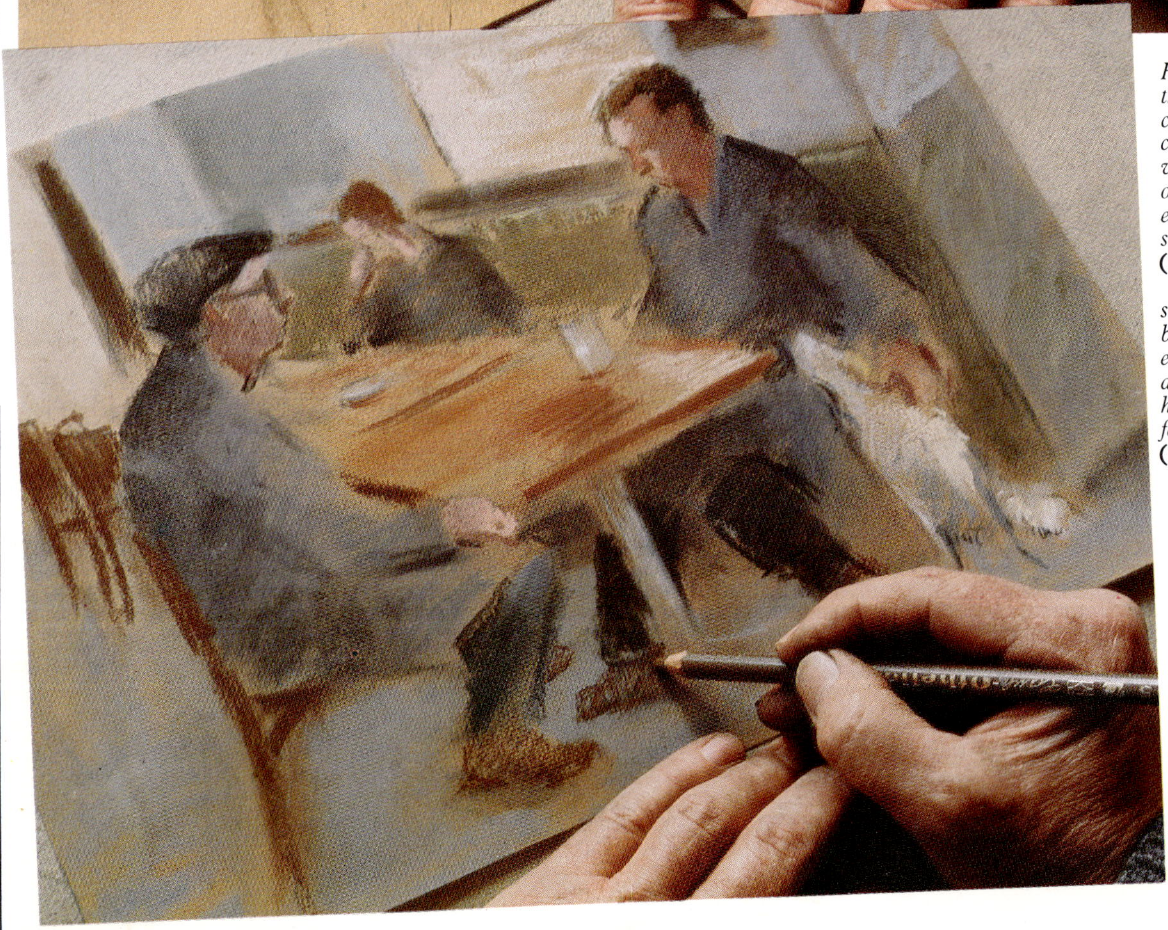

Here the artist strengthens the dark areas with charcoal. He also uses the charcoal to add crisp details which help to create a sense of space — sharply defined edges come forward, whilst softer transitions recede **(above)**.

For the mid-tone shadows he uses a dark brown coloured pencil, this enlivens the dark passages, and the sharp point allows him to resolve the detailed forms such as the shoes **(left)**.